The Synagogues
of
New York's Lower East Side

The Synagogues

of

New York's Lower East Side

Photographs by
Jo Renée Fine

Text by
Gerard R. Wolfe

Washington Mews Books
A Division of New York University Press
New York • 1978

Copyright © 1978 by New York University
Library of Congress Catalog Card Number: 75-15126
ISBN: 0-8147-2559-7

Library of Congress Cataloging in Publication Data
Fine, Jo Reneé.
The synagogues of New York's Lower East Side.

   Bibliography: p.
   1. Synagogues–New York (City)   2. Judaism–New
York (City)   3. Jews in New York (City)–History.
4. Lower East Side, New York–History.   I. Wolfe,
Gerard R., 1926-   II. Title.
BM225.N49F46   296.6'5'097471   75-15126
ISBN 0-8147-2559-7

Design by Publishing Synthesis, Ltd.

Printed in the United States of America
by General Offset Company, Inc., New York, N.Y.

CONTENTS

Introduction by Harry Golden   vii
Acknowledgments   ix

Part One: THE BACKGROUND   1

The First Schisms   11
Multiplication by Division   15
The Reformers and Traditionalists   18
Growth of the East Side Jewish Community   22
The Era of Mass Immigration   27
Decline of the Lower East Side   34
Chronology of Major Hebrew Congregations   37

Part Two: THE SYNAGOGUES   39

Map of the Lower East Side Synagogues   40
The Great Synagogues   41
The Small Synagogues South of Houston Street   103
Shtieblach   133
Map of the Small Synagogues North of Houston Street   142
The Small Synagogues North of Houston Street   143
Former Synagogues   159

Sources   167
List of Photographs   169

INTRODUCTION

In *The Synagogues of New York's Lower East Side,* Professors Jo Renée Fine and Gerard R. Wolfe give us an overview—in photographs and text—of the history of the Jews in America, and tell us something of the amazing intellectual vitality of the Lower East Side.

I went to P.S. 20 on Rivington Street whose alumni include George Gershwin, Edward G. Robinson, Paul Muni, Jacob K. Javits, Charles Silver, Irving Caesar, and myself. The comparatively speedy entry of the immigrant Jews into the American mainstream had its foundation in the Lower East Side. Education was the key to this story and of the Jews' absorption into the American middle class. Public school principals often kept the doors open and the lights on far into the night to accommodate the hundreds of literary societies and debating clubs that represented an intellectual activism without parallel in the history of our educational system.

The book also tells how Jewish life in Colonial New York revolved around the Sephardic Congregation Shearith Israel. John Mill's map of New York in 1695 pinpoints the Mill Street Synagogue which housed Congregation Shearith Israel, by now in its fifth edifice on Central Park West and West Seventieth Street. It was Gershom Mendes Seixas, the minister of Shearith Israel, who represented the Jewish community at the inauguration of President George Washington.

As the Jews moved into the Lower East Side of Manhattan and into other neighborhoods such as Brooklyn's Williamsburg during the 1880s and 1890s, the Irish and Germans moved out, leaving behind their churches and cemeteries. Frequently a church would be purchased by a Jewish congregation and remodeled as a synagogue. The Norfolk Street Baptist Church, for example, became Congregation Beth Hamedrash Hagodol, and the Holy Trinity Lutheran Church was acquired by the Bedford Avenue *Shul.* Today the process continues, but often in reverse. The former Bnai Menasha Achavas Achim synagogue on East Third Street—a street now inhabited mainly by Puerto Ricans—is now the Iglesia de Dios Pentecostal.

The basic idea of Judaism and Democracy is the notion that the past must be tied to the present. Take the case of James Rivington, the publisher of the *Royal Gazette,* a Tory newspaper printed in New York between 1759 and 1780 which espoused the British cause. Mr. Rivington demanded that Washington, Franklin, and Jefferson be hanged when captured by the British. However, when the English forces surrendered and withdrew from the continent, there was no thought of wiping out the name of Rivington. Instead the Americans gathered up all the back issues of the *Royal Gazette,* bound them carefully and placed them in a public library. Democracy like Judaism has no fear of the past. It is interesting to note that the Number One Tory in America gave his name to the Lower East Side street on which tens of thousands of immigrant Jews lived after entering this country. And on the very site of Rivington's printing plant, the Jews eventually built the *Warshawer Shul.*

We should all be grateful to Professors Fine and Wolfe for producing a valuable and engrossing document whose insightful pictures and prose so admirably obey the Biblical injunction, ". . . and thou shall tell it to thy sons!"

Harry Golden

ACKNOWLEDGMENTS

This work would not have been possible without the cooperation and advice of many friends from the Lower East Side. We are particularly grateful to Israel Ginsberg, journalist and chronicler of the old *East Side News,* who spent many days with us walking though the streets of the neighborhood, filling our heads with local history and folklore; to George Freedman, attorney and civic leader, and director of the Educational Alliance's New Era Lecture Forum, for generously making available to us a collection of newspaper articles he wrote about the Lower East Side; to Moses Weiser, president of Congregation Chasam Sopher, his son, Eugene, and the warmhearted members of the *shul* for being such patient subjects before the camera's lens; to Benjamin Markowitz, voluntary *shammos* of Congregation Khal Adas Jeshurun with Anshe Lubz, for the long days he spent with us on our frequent visits to that magnificent synagogue; and to Carl Schiffer, president of Congregation Beth Haknesseth Mogen Avraham, for the cordial receptions at his *shul.*

We are indebted to the following East Side rabbis who gave so freely of their time to teach us so much: Rabbi Ephraim Oshry, Congregation Beth Hamedrash Hagodol; Rabbi Mordecai Mayer, First Roumanian-American Congregation; Rabbi Elias S. Heftler, Congregation Beth Haknesseth Mogen Avraham; Rabbi Julius G. Neumann, House of Sages; Rabbi Joseph Singer, Congregation Bnai Jacob Anshe Brzezan; and Rabbi Max Kohn; of the former Congregation Anshe Slonim.

In addition, we were fortunate in obtaining information, not available elsewhere, from the Educational Alliance's Project Ezra and from the Synagogue

Rescue Project—two East Side organizations dedicated, respectively, to relieving the social and emotional isolation of the neighborhood's Jewish elderly poor and to rescuing for posterity the sacred and artistic artifacts of the disappearing synagogues.

We are also grateful to Rabbi Moshe Davidowitz for his comments and valuable suggestions on the text. To Samuel Wolfe, a former East Sider, an authority on Jewish customs and history (and father of the coauthor), we owe special recognition for his critical reading of the manuscript and his many helpful recommendations. We were very fortunate, too, in having the linguistic expertise and advice of Jacob Moshief, Adjunct Professor of Semitic Languages at New York University. We are also indebted to Eddie Trieber for providing us with his aesthetic judgment, technical assistance, and darkroom expertise in the completion of the photographs; and to Modernage Custom Darkrooms, Inc. for the outstanding quality of the final prints for reproduction in this book.

For the use of invaluable descriptive material on the early synagogues of New York City in Rachel Wischnitzer's *Synagogue Architecture in the United States,* we wish to thank the Jewish Publication Society of America. Finally, we acknowledge the support and encouragement of the Jewish Museum, and the assistance of the librarians at the YIVO Institute for Jewish Research, the Jewish Theological Seminary, the Yeshiva University Library, and the Rare Judaica section of the New York University Bobst Library.

J. R. F.
G. R. W.

PART ONE

THE BACKGROUND

Nowhere else in America can one find a greater collection of magnificent synagogues in one neighborhood than in New York's Lower East Side. Although the great era of Jewish immigration is now history, and the millions who crowded into the teeming quarter have departed, many of their impressive houses of worship still remain. Proud edifices even today, they reflect the heritage, the vibrant religious experience, and the aspirations of a people who came to the land of promise in search of a new life and established the largest Jewish community in the world.

The synagogue not only enriched the religious and cultural life of the immigrant Jew, but offered him solace and respite from his burdensome daily existence. It was in his *shul* that he could relax and meet his friends from the old country, enjoy the golden voice of some cantorial master, and through his devotion, come close to God.

Some of these synagogues are architectural treasures, still cared for with loving-kindness by their dwindling congregations; others, tended by a mere handful of aged and poor worshipers, bear poignant witness to the ravages of time, neglect, and vandalism. And here and there among the dilapidated tenements stand the gaunt ruins of once opulent synagogues, long since abandoned and forgotten.

What is the story of these splendid relics of a bygone era and of the community which first breathed life into them? For the history of these Lower East Side synagogues, we must first go back to the mid-seventeenth century and the arrival of the first Jewish immigrants in New York.

Early on a bright September morning in 1654, a French frigate, said to be the *St. Charles,* arrived in the harbor of New Amsterdam from the West Indies. Among its passengers were twenty-three Spanish and Portuguese Jews—four men, two women, and seventeen children—refugees from Brazil.

The new arrivals were descendants of Jews expelled from the Iberian peninsula during the Inquisition in the 1490s. At that time, a considerable number of Marranos, forcibly converted Jews who practiced Judaism in secret, sailed to the New World with the conquistadores and settled along the east coast of South America. Other Jews, escaping conversion, had fled to the Italian peninsula, to towns in Germany, and to Constantinople. After 1590, when the Spanish yoke was lifted from Holland, then called the United Provinces, many more refugee Jews found a haven in Amsterdam. When Holland captured Brazil from the Portuguese in 1630, the Marranos joyfully returned to their former religious practices; they also established close ties with their brethren in Amsterdam, many of whom sailed to Brazil to join them. A large Jewish community sprang up in Recife, the capital, and also in what is now Surinam and the Dutch Antilles.

The prosperity of the embryonic Jewish community in Brazil was short-lived however, as the colony was recaptured by Portugal in 1654, and all Dutch subjects, including the Jews, were given three months to dispose of their possessions and leave or remain subject to Portuguese rule and the laws of the still-active Inquisition. Most Jews chose to go to Amsterdam, including the twenty-three, who arrived instead, in *New* Amsterdam.

Their intended voyage to Holland from Recife was interrupted a few days out at sea when a marauding Spanish ship seized their vessel. Certain disaster for the Jews was averted a few days later when the French frigate, *St. Charles,* overtook the galleon, forced its surrender, and freed the Jewish prisoners. The French captain then sailed to a port in the West Indies, thought to be Martinique, where the Jews contracted with him to transport them to Amsterdam. They pledged collectively to pay a fee of twenty-five hundred guilders for the voyage, a sum which at today's exchange would be equivalent to about one thousand dollars.

Why Captain de la Motthe deceived them by sailing instead to New Amsterdam is a mystery, for the sum was certainly enough to pay for the trip to Holland. Nevertheless, on that September morning the twenty-three Jews found their ship anchored not in the Amstel River, but in the Hudson. These five families were the first Jews to set foot in North America, except for a Jacob Barsimson who had arrived from Holland one month before.

The Jews' arrival in New Amsterdam was anything but auspicious. They still owed a considerable balance to the French captain for their passage, and their status as Dutch citizens was challenged by Peter Stuyvesant, the colony's governor general. They were, however, granted permission to remain for a while until relatives in Holland could send money to pay off their debts. In the meantime, they auctioned off most of their remaining possessions to obtain food and shelter, although it is said that many of the Dutch burghers gave back the Jews' personal effects after purchasing them. While they were waiting for the ship to return from Holland, the weather turned cold. The twenty-three "temporary" immigrants, unaccustomed to the climate, suffered greatly in the months that followed.

Governor Stuyvesant was most anxious to be rid of them, and within a few days of their arrival he sent off a letter to the Dutch West India Company, which controlled the colony: "The Jews who have arrived would nearly all like to remain here, but learning that they—with their customary usury and deceitful trading with Christians—were very repugnant, and fearing that owing to their present indigence they might become a charge in the coming winter, we have deemed it useful to require them in a friendly way to depart; praying most seriously that the deceitful race be not allowed further to infect and trouble this new colony."

The reply from the directors of the company, which did not arrive until the following April, seven months after the Jews' arrival, must have staggered Stuyvesant, for not only was his petition denied, but the letter also granted permission for the Jews to stay on and engage in commerce, "provided they did not become a burden on the community."

Stuyvesant then devised a series of restrictive acts against the Jews, prohibiting them from travelling, from trading in the land between the North and South (Hudson and Delaware) rivers, from conducting retail business, and from the public practice of their religion. Again, the leaders of the Jewish community sent an appeal to the Dutch West India Company. A few months later a strong letter came back to Governor Stuyvesant overruling all but his last restriction. What the governor overlooked, or was unaware of, was that a large number of stockholders of the company were influential Dutch Jews.

Although Peter Stuyvesant appeared to have a special animosity toward Jews, his dislikes were not reserved exclusively for them. Recently arrived Lutherans were also forbidden to worship publicly, and the Quakers were singled out for particularly repressive measures. In 1662, Stuyvesant imprisoned John Bowne, a

Quaker from Flushing, for permitting "that abominable sect" to hold a prayer meeting in his house. Bowne was later banished and made his way to Holland, where he pleaded so effectively for liberty of conscience that the Amsterdam chamber of the West India Company issued an edict declaring that "the consciences of men, at least, ought to remain free and unshackled."

Two key events helped raise the status of Jews in New Amsterdam and gain them virtual equal rights. Soon after their arrival in the colony, Asser Levy and Jacob Barsimson sought the right to perform guard duty instead of having to pay the tax imposed on Jews as a substitute for not being permitted to stand guard. After correspondence with the Dutch West India Company, Levy and Barsimon's petition was granted, and the two were permitted to join the citizen guard. Two years later in 1657, Levy responded to a public notice which announced that any resident who wished to be granted burgher (citizen) status must apply to the burgomasters of the city. He claimed that since he had been performing guard service and possessed a burgher certificate from the city of Amsterdam, citizen status ought not be refused him. The burgomasters denied his application, and he appealed directly to Governor Stuyvesant. Surprisingly, the governor granted both this request and, soon afterward, a similar appeal for citizen's rights from a number of the town's leading Jews.

The number of Jews in the colony remained quite small for the next ten years. Earlier, a few did arrive from Amsterdam, among them Abraham de Lucena, bringing the first Torah scroll to North America. After the English seized New Amsterdam in 1664, a trickle of Jewish immigrants arrived, both from England and the West Indies, and even from France. But by the end of the seventeenth century, New York's Jewish population still numbered no more than one hundred. A small Jewish community was established in Newport, Rhode Island, but it did not thrive until at least half a century later. Within a few years after the turn of the century, substantial Jewish communities were established in Philadelphia, Richmond, Savannah, and Charleston (which was the largest), bringing the total Jewish population in the North American colonies to approximately two thousand.

One of the first petitions of the newly established Jewish community was a request for a piece of land to be used as a burial ground. After about a year's delay, permission was granted by the local authorities to use a small plot outside the city limits. The precise location of this cemetery is no longer known, but a second tract of ground was purchased in 1682 and enlarged in 1729. A substantial section still exists today on St. James Place, just south of Chatham Square. This first cemetery of the Spanish and Portuguese Synagogue, now a national historic landmark, is the oldest artifact on Manhattan Island, and is still maintained by the same congregation. In the belief that the dead are to be respected, the Spanish and Portuguese Synagogue has steadfastly refused to sell any of its cemetery holdings. The first interment is thought to be that of Benjamin Bueno de Mesquita in 1683, just one year after he arranged for the purchase of the land.

Among other burials are eighteen Jewish soldiers from the Revolutionary War, whose grave markers were dedicated in 1932 by the Daughters of the American Revolution; Abraham de Lucena, the congregation's second *hazzan,* or minister, and Gershom Mendes Seixas, the first American-born minister, who helped rebuild the Jewish community after the Revolutionary War, and who also served as a trustee of Columbia College and represented the Jewish community at the inauguration of President George Washington. The little cemetery also figured in the defense of the city in 1776, just after the outbreak of the Revolution, when General Charles Lee mounted two batteries of cannon among the tombstones to help cover Washington's retreat up Manhattan Island.

The Spanish and Portuguese Synagogue–Congregation Shearith Israel (or Remnant of Israel), also maintains two other small cemeteries in Manhattan. The second (actually the third, counting the lost first burial ground), on West Eleventh Street in what is now Greenwich Village, was built in 1805 as the city spread northward; a third on Twenty-first Street, just west of Sixth Avenue, was opened in 1829. Since 1851, the congregation has been using a cemetery in the Cypress Hills section of Brooklyn.

Until the beginning of the eighteenth century, a majority of the Jews in New York were Sephardic (from the Hebrew word for Spain, *Sepharad),* descendants of Jews who lived in the Iberian peninsula prior to their expulsion during the Inquisition in 1492. The immigrants who came to America during the eighteenth century and afterward, however, were mostly Ashkenazic (from the old Hebrew word for Germany, *Ashkenaz).*

The Ashkenazic Jews originally settled in Germany during the Middle Ages and developed their own Judeo-Germanic language and culture. In the following centuries, many migrated to eastern Europe, settling in what is now Poland, Russia, Lithuania, Hungary, and Rumania. Their wanderings through eastern Europe were hastened by the dread Bogdan Chmielnicki massacres in Poland in 1648, during which some Jews found their way back to Germany. The first Ashkenazic Jews to arrive in America were mainly from Germany (with some from Holland and England), but only a trickle came from Poland and Russia.

The Sephardic Jews spoke Portuguese as their day-to-day language, although most knew Spanish as well and used it as their commercial language and for translating the Bible. The Spanish spoken by the Sephardim from the eastern Mediterranean (who arrived in the early twentieth century) was called Ladino. It included many words from Hebrew and other languages and was written in Hebrew script.

The Ashkenazic Jews, on the other hand, were mostly German-speaking. Although there were no basic differences in religious beliefs, the Ashkenazim were more fundamentalist in religious practices, their liturgical ritual was not the same, their pronunciation of Hebrew followed different rules, and their way of life was even more divergent. The newly arrived Ashkenazim could not understand the sympathy shown by the Sephardim toward the outside world, nor could they adjust to what must have seemed the almost total assimilation by the Sephardim into the developing American society. As the established group, the Sephardic Jews were active in political affairs, and many had achieved considerable status in commerce, the professions, and the arts. Yet in spite of these linguistic, social, cultural, and ritualistic differences, the Sephardim and Ashkenazim in New York lived together in relative harmony, frequently intermarrying and sharing until 1825 the same house of worship.

At the time of their arrival in America, the Jews were forced to hold their services in secret. Later, in 1682, under a somewhat more tolerant British rule, they conducted their first organized services in a rented room on Beaver Street and founded Congregation Shearith Israel (Remnant of Israel). A short time afterward they moved to the upper floor of a windmill at the corner of Mill Lane and Mill Street (now South William Street). The old flour mill is long since gone, but the huge millstones are still preserved in the present Spanish and Portuguese Synagogue on Central Park West.

In 1729 a plot of land was purchased just south of the mill for the construction of the first synagogue building in North America. The sale price was one hundred pounds plus one loaf of sugar and one pound of tea. Completed the following year, Congregation Shearith Israel's synagogue was a small one-story masonry building thirty-five feet square and twenty-one feet high with tall arched windows topped by a peaked roof. A women's gallery ran the length of the three side walls. Adjacent to the synagogue was a schoolhouse, a *mikveh* (ritual bath), and a water pump. No trace of the buildings remains today, except for a plaque at 26 South William Street, but a number of the synagogue's artifacts are displayed in Shearith Israel's building.

On a visit to New York in 1812, the Reverend John Pierce, a Congregationalist minister from Brookline, Massachusetts, attended a Saturday service at the Mill Street synagogue, and wrote the following description in his diary: "I attended the worship of the Jews in their synagogue in company with the Rev. Timo. Alden. The men occupy the lower floor. The women are in the gallery, which has a breastwork as high as their chins. The men wore white sashes; had wax candles burning and went with great ceremony to the altar to take out a scroll on which was written their law. Their exercises consisting of prayers and singing from the Psalms and recitations from the Law were performed by young and old altogether in the Hebrew language. They were very attentive to me, and finding that we could read Hebrew, they pointed out to us the places from which their services were taken."

The arrival of Jewish immigrants from Europe was temporarily stopped by the American Revolution. Among the Jews of New York, the majority sided with the patriots. Most noteworthy was Haym Solomon, a businessman and broker, who was responsible for raising a considerable amount of the money needed both to finance the American Revolution and to save the new nation from collapse later on. Arriving in the city from Poland in 1772, he quickly joined the Sons of Liberty and was an outspoken freedom fighter. The British arrested him as a spy, but later freed him, and he subsequently helped many American and French prisoners to escape. Again sought by the British, he escaped to Philadelphia. Although Solomon arrived in this land penniless, his highly successful brokerage business raised over two hundred thousand dollars which he loaned to help finance the rebellion. He was later familiarly known as the "broker to the Office of Finance of the United States." The United States never repaid Haym Solomon, but in 1975 it did issue a commemorative postage stamp honoring his contribution to the cause of liberty.

Another Jewish patriot was Gershom Mendes Seixas, the first American-born minister of Congregation Shearith Israel. The term "minister" was applied by the congregation to its *hazzan,* or chief religious official; the term nowadays is applied only to the cantor. There was no ordained rabbi in America until the mid-nineteenth century. Seixas went into voluntary exile and left New York City rather than remain and be forced to collaborate with the British army of occupation. He and a number of fellow congregants departed in secret, carrying with them the sacred scrolls of the Mill Street synagogue. After his return in 1783, Seixas resumed his role as spiritual leader of the Jewish community of New York and was its representative at Washington's inauguration. One of the Torah scrolls left behind in the synagogue was desecrated by a few drunken British soldiers. No longer usable, it is still preserved as a historic memento in the present Shearith Israel archives.

By 1800 the Jewish population of New York City had grown to about four hundred, most of them Ashkenazim. Yet, Shearith Israel clung tightly to its Sephardic *minhag* (ritual), which was not surprising, since the minority patrician Sephardim were the established leaders of the Jewish community, for they *were* the first to arrive; and the Sephardim were also accustomed to organized religious activities without rabbinical leadership (there still were no rabbis in America—the *hazzan* was the spiritual head of the community). At the same time, the Ashkenazic members tended to be more cosmopolitan and tolerant than their brethren in Europe, and faced with the cataclysm of the American Revolution and the need to maintain a solid front to the outside world, they managed to settle their differences in private. In 1818 the Mill Street synagogue was enlarged to accommodate the growing congregation.

Within the next twenty-five years a small but steady stream of Ashkenazic immigrants settled in the city, mostly from Germany, Holland, and Poland. They were much poorer, more traditionalist, and less worldly, and they found the rituals of their assimilated coreligionists—both the Sephardim and the established Ashkenazim—strange and hard to accept. They made several requests of Shearith Israel's board of trustees to permit them to conduct their own separate services, but they were flatly denied. Fearing the growing influence of the new Ashkenazic immigrants, the trustees tightened the rules of membership—contrary to the New York State Religious Societies Corporation Law of 1784, which provided that any seat holder in a religious institution who paid dues for one year automatically became an elector. Declaring that membership was a privilege, not a right, the trustees, in 1825, arrogated to the electors the authority to approve a prospective member of the congregation. In September, a group of sixteen Ashkenazic Jews applied for membership, but only two were accepted. Tensions increased, and the established Ashkenazic Jews suddenly found themselves in the middle of the conflict.

The last straw came with a very minor incident in which an Ashkenazic member, Barrow E. Cohen, refused to give the customary two-shilling donation when he was called to read from the Torah during a service. Summoned before the board of trustees for a hearing, he denied being aware of the requirement and angrily threatened to seek redress in civil court. He was backed by the influential Haym Solomon, who then resigned from the board in protest. Ultimately, Cohen was exonerated by the trustees, who also withdrew the requirement for the donation. However, the board sent him a letter of admonition which he refused to accept. Infuriated by what they considered an act of contempt, the board convened a general meeting of the congregation, at which it was decided that Cohen would be barred from any future readings of the Torah and would be prevented from receiving any further honor.

THE FIRST SCHISMS

The leaders of the dissident Ashkenazim then called a meeting at Washington Hall, 533 Pearl Street, and voted to secede from Congregation Shearith Israel. They gave as their reasons (1) the basic desire of their group to adhere to the Ashkenazic rite, (2) the need for a new and larger synagogue building to replace the small Mill Street synagogue, and (3) the remoteness of Mill Street from the homes of most of the congregants. Although not openly expressed, a decisive factor in the schism was the intransigence of Shearith Israel in the face of mounting complaints against its strict controls and formalities. And in retrospect, one cannot but speculate that the Ashkenazim's desire for freedom from authority must have had some of its roots in the successful American Revolution of fifty years earlier.

The group then arranged to purchase at a foreclosure sale the two-year-old African Presbyterian Mission Church at 119 Elm (now Lafayette) Street. Thus, Congregation Bnai Jeshurun (Sons of Israel) became New York City's first Ashkenazic synagogue, adopting the Ashkenazic *minhag* (ritual) of the Great Synagogue of London. The first Ashkenazic congregation in America, founded in 1797 in Philadelphia by German Jews, was called the Hebrew–German Society Rodeph Shalom.

Relations between the breakaway group and Shearith Israel were somewhat cool at first, but the trustees of the Mill Street congregation did lend them four Torah scrolls for the dedication of the new synagogue and even sent officials to attend the ceremony and give their blessing. However, what Shearith Israel had feared most— the division of the Jewish community—had finally come to pass.

The new Elm Street synagogue created somewhat of a sensation in the local press, with many engravings of the former church building and glowing descriptions of the new furnishings. The exterior was designed in the style of a

Roman temple and the structure was topped with an incongruous Gothic-style steeple. In the 1828 edition of *The Picture of New York,* the interior was described as being finished "in a rich and neat style." The description goes on to say: "A row of pillars supports the gallery, which has a railing of carved mahogany. The reading desk, which stands in the centre, facing east, is of mahogany, enclosed within a railing of fret work. The Ark, on the east side of the church, is large and circular, of curled maple and mahogany, with a dome supported with Ionic columns, with caps and bases. The Ten Commandments in front are of raised golden letters on white marble, supported by gold cornucopias. In front of the holy receptacle of the law hangs a rich curtain of blue satin, elegantly embroidered with Hebrew inscriptions. The centre chandelier, together with four smaller ones and clusters of astral lamps over the gallery, with the candelabras, are richly furnished with bronze and gold, the whole being splendid and in good taste."

Nine years later, in 1834, Congregation Shearith Israel abandoned its Mill Street synagogue downtown and erected a new building further uptown at 60 Crosby Street, not far from the Lower East Side. They brought with them a number of artifacts from the old synagogue, including the *almembar,* or *bimah* (reader's platform), the railing that surrounded the *almembar,* four candlesticks, a Spanish brass candleholder, a wine goblet, a spice box, two brass urns, and a set of Ten-Commandment tablets—all of which can be seen today in a colonial-style chapel within the present Spanish and Portuguese Synagogue.

The new building was designed by the noted architect Robert Mook in the then fashionable Greek Revival style and was illuminated by gas. Surrounding the synagogue was a small yard which gave access to the residence of the *hazzan* (minister) and the *shammos* (sexton). According to contemporary accounts, the Crosby Street synagogue's interior was "finished in a style of simple and remarkable elegance." There was the traditional gallery for women; and the furnishings of the sanctuary, including the Ark itself which held the Torah scrolls, were of mahogany and satinwood. A basement chapel, equipped with benches from the old Mill Street synagogue, was used for weekday services. Adjoining the chapel was a school room and meeting room. The congregation remained on Crosby Street until 1860, when new and better neighborhoods were started further uptown, and it moved to a site at 5 West Nineteenth Street, off Fifth Avenue.

Most of the wealthier Jews, particularly the Sephardim, had long since abandoned the crowded lower Manhattan neighborhood and moved to Greenwich Village and to the streets west of Broadway and north of Canal Street. The less affluent Jews tended to settle along Baxter and Bayard streets, the neighborhood which late in the nineteenth century became Chinatown. With the opening of the Bnai Jeshurun Synagogue, many Ashkenazic Jews found it convenient to move across the Bowery into a semirural area, which is now the Lower East Side.

Until well into the eighteenth century the East Side was a tranquil suburb northeast of the city. The land had been part of the estates of the Rutgers, De Lancey, and Stuyvesant families until its development as a residential area after the Revolutionary War. Henry Rutgers, a captain in the Colonial Army whose name is honored by the state university of New Jersey, reaped a handsome profit from the sale of his property, as did the descendants of the Dutch Governor, Peter Stuyvesant. James De Lancey, on the other hand, did not fare so well. He chose the wrong side in the Revolution and afterward suffered the fate of many Tories, the confiscation of all his landholdings. De Lancey is remembered today only in the name of the Lower East Side's major thoroughfare, Delancey Street, which in a final indignity, misspells his name.

As Shearith Israel moved further away geographically from Bnai Jeshurun and the nearby Lower East Side, it also separated itself philosophically, and its contact with the Ashkenazim diminished. In the years that followed the schism, there were only occasional alliances, such as in the founding of the Jews' Hospital in the City of New York (later, Mount Sinai Hospital) and in the establishment by Shearith Israel of a number of charitable and educational institutions among the later immigrant Jews of the Lower East Side. But for all the rest, the separation was final. It is interesting to note that after the secession of Bnai Jeshurun, there were no further defections from Shearith Israel; yet within a few short years a chain of events would occur which would shatter the unity of the Ashkenazic community.

Meanwhile, Bnai Jeshurun, now on its own as New York's second Hebrew congregation, faced the future with uncertainty. One of the first problems to be settled was that of a burial ground. Since Shearith Israel denied the fledgling group use of its cemetery on West Eleventh Street, Bnai Jeshurun was forced to purchase its own land, choosing a site at West Thirty-second Street near Sixth Avenue. Interments were made there for the next quarter of a century, until 1851 when the city banned all burials south of Eighty-sixth Street. The congregation then managed to come to an agreement with Shearith Israel, and the two shared in the acquisition of cemetery land in the Cypress Hills section of Brooklyn.

The burial question was minor in comparison with the problems of succeeding years. At the time of secession, the membership of Bnai Jeshurun consisted mainly of two groups of Ashkenazim. One was well established, assimilated, and spoke English as well as some Yiddish; the other consisted of poorer recent arrivals from

13

Germany and Poland, all either German- or Yiddish-speaking, who had little in common, socially or economically, with their fellow Ashkenzim. As new immigrants arrived, the Americanized congregants of Bnai Jeshurun soon found themselves in the minority. Substantial differences developed between them, for the newcomers represented what seemed an almost primitive way of life and a contrasting form of fundamentalist Orthodox ritual.

In 1828, a group of German, Dutch, and Polish Jews decided to break away from Bnai Jeshurun and found their own congregation. These were relatively recent immigrants, mostly of low economic status, living close together in the Chatham Square area—a miniature Jewish community on such nearby streets as Centre, White, and Pearl, and particularly in "Jews' Alley"—a small section of Madison Street between Oliver and James streets, adjacent to the old first Shearith Israel cemetery. They rented a meeting room at 202½ Grand Street and named their new congregation Anshe Chesed (People of Kindness), thus becoming the first congregation to locate in the Lower East Side. Eight years later the growing membership demanded larger quarters, and space was acquired above the New York Dispensary, at White and Centre streets. Shortly afterward, the growing congregation purchased a small Quaker Meeting House at 38 Henry Street, where they remained until 1850, when they dedicated their new synagogue building on Norfolk Street.

Meanwhile, Bnai Jeshurun suffered another secession in 1835, albeit a brief one. The separation occurred when a number of Polish congregants were angered over a trivial disagreement with the trustees. A young man wishing to marry the daughter of the president of Bnai Jeshurun requested that his prospective father-in-law, John I. Hart, perform the ceremony. For whatever reasons, the trustees refused, and the bridegroom-to-be and his friends withdrew and formed a new congregation, Ohavey Zedek (Lovers of Righteousness). The new organization did not last however, and in three months all members were back in the fold of Bnai Jeshurun.

Four years later, in 1839, a crisis developed. For over a year, a debate had been raging about the admission fees charged to new members. Many congregants felt that this was an effective way of excluding the poorer applicants. A compromise was offered by the trustees, reducing the fee to a nominal five dollars, but still there were strong objections. Whether or not this was the real reason or just a cause célèbre, a group of German-speaking Poles, mostly from the city of Posen (now Poznan), formally withdrew from Bnai Jeshurun to organize their own congregation, Shaarey Zedek (Gates of Righteousness). It is likely that there were other motives, one of which was doubtless the desire for members from the same European community to remain together, free from the domination of the more assimilated Jews.

MULTIPLICATION BY DIVISION

At about the same time, another group of Polish Jews resigned from the eleven-year-old Anshe Chesed congregation and joined the newborn Shaarey Zedek. The new congregation, like its predecessor, Anshe Chesed, first used rented rooms. The actual year of organization is not clear; some authorities claim it was 1839, others say it was 1837. In any case, Shaarey Zedek soon outgrew its space at 472 Pearl Street, near Chatham Square, and moved to a location at City Hall Place. Then, in 1840, they obtained the popular meeting rooms which had recently been used by Anshe Chesed above the New York Dispensary. This space had also been used by Shearith Israel in 1835 while they were awaiting the completion of their Crosby Street synagogue. Membership in Shaarey Zedek swelled when the congregation made it known that they would accept families which had intermarried, a phenomenon that had become the source of great concern to the Jewish community after the Revolutionary War. Remaining above the Dispensary for ten years, Shaarey Zedek again followed Anshe Chesed and purchased the small Quaker Church at 38 Henry Street which its sister congregation had been using, becoming the second congregation to locate in the Lower East Side.

The year 1839 witnessed another important secession. A group of German Jews from Anshe Chesed united to organize a new congregation, moving to an apartment in a private house at 122 Attorney Street on the Lower East Side. Services were conducted exclusively in German, except for the required Hebrew liturgy, and as such, the newly-formed Congregation Shaarey Hashamayim (Gates of Heaven) became the first of a large number of German-speaking congregations to settle in the neighborhood. The Lower East Side was then largely a German-Gentile area (with some Irish as well), and with the steady influx of the German-Jewish population, the area from around Grand Street north to Fourteenth Street soon earned the name of *klein Deutschland.* However, when the great waves of east European Jewish immigration began sweeping into the Lower East Side in the 1880s, both German-speaking communities fled uptown—the Jews to Harlem, and the Gentiles to Yorkville.

Congregation Shaarey Hashamayim remained on the East Side until 1898 when it joined with Congregation Ahavath Chesed (Lovers of Kindness, or Mercy) which had left the Lower East Side some years before and was now at Lexington Avenue and East Fifty-Fifth Street. The combined congregations adopted their present name, Central Synagogue, in 1920 (See page 23).

Meanwhile, a few doors up from Shaarey Hashamayim in a private house at 156 Attorney Street, another breakaway group of German Jews who were disenchanted with the leadership of Congregation Anshe Chesed founded Congregation Rodeph Shalom (Pursuers of Peace) in 1842.

In the same year, Congregation Shaarey Zedek experienced *its* first division. Dissatisfied with the domination by Germans of synagogue affairs, a group of Poles and Russians formed their own congregation which they called Beth Israel (House of Israel). They located in a meeting house at 70 Leonard Street, and a short time later moved to rooms on Centre Street, between Pearl and Duane streets. In 1850, they acquired the favored space above the New York Dispensary, formerly used by Anshe Chesed, Shearith Israel, and Shaarey Zedek.

This pattern of multiplication by division of the newly organized houses of worship continued with the founding in 1845 of Congregation Shaarey Tefilah (Gates of Prayer) by a group of assimilated English Jews. As former members of Bnai Jeshurun, they feared the growing power of the German-speaking majority, and they decided to organize their own congregation when the trustees enacted what the English Jews felt were restrictive membership laws, similar to those passed by Shearith Israel twenty years before. They objected strenuously to the requirement that only the electors of the synagogue could propose someone for membership, regardless of whether or not the prospective member had been paying his dues and attending regularly. The trustees further decreed that membership in Bnai Jeshurun would be granted only after a two-thirds vote of the general membership, of whom more than two-thirds were German-speaking. In addition, services were conducted exclusively in German, contrary to the wishes of the English-speaking Jews.

The newly formed Shaarey Tefilah met temporarily at 67 Franklin Street and immediately contracted for the construction of its own synagogue building. It should be remembered that in 1845 there were only two synagogue buildings in the entire city—Shearith Israel on Crosby Street and Bnai Jeshurun in its converted church on Elm Street. For its new house of worship, it was appropriate that the leaders of Shaarey Tefilah should select as one of the two designers Leopold Eidlitz, the first Jewish architect in the United States. The building, in an early

Romanesque Revival style, was erected at 112 Wooster Street, and dedicated in 1847. Before its completion, the *hazzan,* Samuel Meyer Isaacs described it in the August 1846 edition of the Jewish publication *The Occident* in these glowing terms: "The imposing grandeur of the style, together with its Oriental origin, its deep shadows, bold projections, noble columns, and lofty arches, will render it best adapted for a building of this class and character."

Writing in the August 1847 issue of the same publication, editor Isaac Leeser was somewhat less enthusiastic: "The style of the building is so new to us and so little idea had we of the interior arrangements that we have not yet been able to make up our mind whether to approve it for a synagogue or not. But there can be no question that it is a beautiful structure."

This third New York synagogue was indeed a beautiful building, with original stained-glass panels, a marble base for the reader's platform, a balcony for choir and musicians, an ornate Gothic style rose window, heavy oak furnishings, and an Ark platform of Italian marble. Unfortunately, the striking building no longer stands. Twenty-two years later in 1869 the congregation built an imposing synagogue uptown on West Forty-fourth Street, designed by Jewish architect Henry Fernbach. It was an imposing Lombard–Gothic style edifice topped by a huge Oriental dome, with minaret-like pinnacles. It, too, has long since disappeared.

By 1847 there were about thirteen thousand Jews in New York—a little over three percent of the city's population. In the previous ten years the number of Jews had leaped more than sixfold as severe turmoil in Europe encouraged the first mass migration of Jews to America. Various German states, particularly Bavaria, had begun imposing severe economic and social restrictions on the Jews. High taxes, for example, made it virtually impossible for Jewish merchants to conduct business; travel was restricted; and to limit the future Jewish population, Bavaria severely regulated the number of Jewish marriages that could be performed. In addition, a general economic slump throughout central Europe further encouraged a steady emigration of German-speaking Jews to America. Although most were from German-speaking areas, many also came from Poland, Bohemia, Hungary, and Russia. When they arrived, they tended to group together, if not by *shtetl* (town), then by common national areas. Except among the German speakers, the Yiddish language was the common linguistic bond between them. In 1848, with the failure of the abortive liberal revolutions throughout Europe, thousands of Jews and non-Jews came to America, the majority of Jews settling in the Lower East Side.

It should be remembered that in spite of all the secessions and mergers among the various houses of worship, all the congregations remained strictly Orthodox. Yet there were changes in the wind.

THE REFORMERS AND TRADITIONALISTS

With the arrival in New York of highly educated, upper-class German Jews, the desire for a change of religious practices came into the open. This movement for reform had its roots in several German communities, especially in Hamburg, where many Jewish congregations pushed for a rather drastic alteration of the ritual "to dignify the services, to worship more meaningfully, to involve the rising generation of young people, and to occupy a position of greater respect among the non-Jewish community." Many objected to the rather loud, "undisciplined" traditional Ashkenazic service in Hebrew, with chanting to melodies that were non-Western and alien to them. Since the prayers were conducted in Hebrew, which was considered a sacred language, many of the German Jews repeated them by rote but did not understand them. They therefore sought a liturgy which would be comprehensible as well as uplifting. Another objection was to the lack of preaching by the rabbi. Customarily, the rabbi preaches a sermon only twice a year (on the Sabbath before Passover and on the Sabbath during the High Holidays, on *Shabbat Shuva,* the Sabbath between Rosh Hashanah and Yom Kippur), and then usually on some Talmudic point.

In America, Shearith Israel did have regular sermons in English, but in other respects, it clung to its dignified Orthodoxy. Bnai Jeshurun's *hazzan,* Samuel Meyer Isaacs (later of Shaarey Tefilah), introduced English in 1840, and he was followed in 1849 by the English *hazzan,* Morris J. Raphall, whose brilliant oratorical fame was widespread.

A society called the Cultus Verein was formed in 1844, advocating drastic changes in the ritual and customs. Among its members was Dr. Leo Merzbacher, recently arrived from Germany and the first ordained rabbi to come to America. Until that time, the spiritual leader of each congregation was the *hazzan.* Since under Jewish law, every Jew must be knowledgeable about the Talmud and traditions, being ordained is not required. In fact, a prayer service, or *minyan,* may be conducted by any group of at least ten adult males, without the leadership of a

18

rabbi. Dr. Merzbacher was engaged by both Congregations Anshe Chesed and Rodeph Shalom, but his tenure was terminated the following year when he spoke out against the Orthodox custom in which women shave their heads before marriage and thereafter wear a *shaitel,* or ritual wig.

The second ordained rabbi to come to America was Dr. Max Lilienthal, who arrived from Munich in 1845. The following year, he was elected rabbi of the three most important German synagogues, Anshe Chesed, Rodeph Shalom, and Shaarey Hashamayim, and he divided his duties equally between the three congregations. These three houses of worship formed the nucleus of the influential United German Jewish Community, a federation of German-speaking congregations. Dr. Lilienthal, one of the foremost educators of his time, struggled to unite the efforts of the three synagogues to establish day schools, and by 1847 he was in charge of the newly formed Union School, the largest and most well-run Jewish school in the country, with over two hundred fifty youngsters in attendance.

The Cultus Verein was one of a number of Reform societies which sprang up among the German Jews in America and which later became the nuclei of new "temples," as the reformers called them. The Cultus Verein organized its own congregation, which it named Temple Emanu-El (literally, God Is with Us). In April 1845, the organization rented quarters in a house at the corner of Grand and Clinton streets, which it occupied for two years, with Dr. Merzbacher as the first rabbi.

Few congregations were wealthy enough to afford the construction of a new synagogue building, and it was far less expensive to remodel an existing building. As many Protestant congregations moved out of the Lower East Side, their church buildings were purchased by Hebrew congregations for conversion to synagogues. Bnai Jeshurun acquired the Elm Street Presbyterian church, for example, and Anshe Chesed, and later Shaarey Zedek, purchased the Quaker Meeting House on Henry Street. In 1847 Temple Emanu-El bought a Methodist church at 56 Chrystie Street and engaged architect Leopold Eidlitz to supervise the reconstruction and design appropriate interior furnishings. At its dedication, the term "temple" was officially adopted, beginning a tradition in America for Reform synagogues, and later for many Conservative synagogues as well.

The Temple, as the synagogue came to be known, remained at the site until 1854, when the congregation moved uptown to Twelfth Street, east of Fourth Avenue, in the uppermost reaches of the Lower East Side. Their former Chrystie Street building was then sold to the Polish congregation Beth Israel, which in the

19

past months had been using the popular rooms above the New York Dispensary. The much used building was ultimately demolished, along with its neighboring tenements, to make way for the construction of the new Manhattan Bridge just after the turn of the century. The new building was a former Baptist church, and the congregation again called on Leopold Eidlitz to do the remodeling. Following the tenets of Reform Judaism, there was no separate gallery for women, and the pulpit and reader's desk were placed directly in front of the Ark. The Gothic-style Ark, together with glass Ten-Commandment tablets were brought from the Chrystie Street temple and were set into the apse. When Temple Emanu-El moved uptown to Fifth Avenue and Forty-third Street in 1868, it again contracted with Eidlitz, this time to erect the largest synagogue building in the world. (In its move up Fifth Avenue to East 65th Street in 1929, Temple Emanu-El again erected the largest Jewish house of worship in the world.)

Among the extensive changes proposed by the reformers were broad revisions and shortening of the prayer service and prayer books; the abolition of the one-year cycle of Torah reading; the substitution of the word "confirmation" for *bar mitzvah* (extending the ceremony to girls, as well; the introduction of instrumental music and the singing of German hymns; the discontinuance of the practices of using the *talith* (prayer shawl) and *tefillin* (phylacteries), of segregating women, and of wearing a hat indoors. Rabbi Isaac Mayer Wise, the most important exponent of Reform Judaism in America, came to this country from Bohemia in 1846 to serve as a rabbi in Albany. He founded the Hebrew Union College in Cincinnati and the Union of American Hebrew Congregations, and after a meeting with a group of New York rabbis in 1847, undertook the publication of a modernized Hebrew prayer book which he hoped would be used in all American synagogues, *Minhag America* (American Ritual), to replace the Sephardic and Ashkenazic rituals. Later, it was Rabbi David Einhorn from Bavaria who helped develop the theoretical foundation for the Reform movement. In the early 1860s he was chosen as rabbi of a new congregation, Adas Jeshurun (Community of Israel), about which little is known.

By the mid-eighteen fifties, Temple Emanu-El and Shaarey Tefilah had surpassed all other congregations in leadership, even Shearith Israel and Bnai Jeshurun, so popular had the Reform movement become. Emanu-El, particularly, rose not only in influence, but in financial and social position as well. As a latecomer (1845) in the family of New York synagogues, its meteoric rise, abetted by the power of the German community, was most unusual.

Soon after the founding of Temple Emanu-El, Congregation Anshe Chesed, formerly a moderate traditionalist group, became New York's second Reform house of worship and commenced construction of its own synagogue building at 172 Norfolk Street. Anshe Chesed was a bit slower in adopting the radical reforms of its neighbor and rival, Temple Emanu-El. The conventional Orthodox prayer book was still used, men wore hats, and women sat in the gallery; however, the *hazzan* now faced the congregation, assisted by a mixed choir of men and women. Later in 1874 the congregation moved uptown, merging with congregation Adas Jeshurun to form Temple Beth El (House of God). The new partners built a synagogue at Lexington Avenue and Sixty-third Street, which remained on the site until 1891 when they moved to a very chic location at Fifth Avenue and Seventy-sixth Street. Again they had a new building erected, this time in Byzantine–Moorish style, which is still remembered by old-timers today. Its imposing iron and glass dome overlooking Central Park was an outstanding landmark, listed in all city guidebooks until 1930 when the building was demolished. Temple Beth El had merged with Temple Emanu-El a few years before, and its name is now recalled in the beautiful Beth El Chapel adjacent to the present Temple Emanu-El's main sanctuary.

As Reform Judaism spread, the breach between adherents of the new movement and the traditional Orthodox groups grew wider. Reform was particularly attractive to the affluent upper-class Jews who were more integrated into the American scene, while the traditionalists dissociated themselves from what they considered nothing less than heresy. Communication between Orthodox and Reform synagogues was virtually nonexistent. The split was widened further in later years, if such was even possible, when some of the Reform temples began conducting services on Sunday. Among the Reform and more moderate German congregations, there was a short-lived movement to unite all German-speaking synagogues and bring under one roof the Congregations Anshe Chesed, Rodeph Shalom, Shaarey Hashamayim, and Temple Emanu-El. But Anshe Chesed and Rodeph Shalom felt that Emanu-El was too avant garde, and withdrew from the proposal. Shaarey Hashamayim, whose Attorney Street meeting rooms were in bad repair, would have benefited most from a union with Emanu-El; but they procrastinated, and after a vote of the membership, also rejected the plan. No further attempt was made to bring the Reform synagogues together until the 1870s, and the only real cooperation among them was the pooling of cemetery facilities for burying the poor.

GROWTH OF THE EAST SIDE JEWISH COMMUNITY

Toward the mid-nineteenth century, other congregations were organized, sometimes the result of mergers or further divisions of existing groups, but mostly from the need for more synagogue facilities to accommodate the increasing number of immigrants. The political upheavals which shook Europe periodically sent thousands of refugees to our shores. Jews were now arriving at the rate of about one thousand per year, a harbinger of the enormous flood of immigrants which would pour into the Lower East Side by the 1880s.

During this important period, the Lower East Side was witness to the birth of one of the most influential Jewish organizations, the Independent Order Bnai Brith (Sons of the Covenant). An outgrowth of the numerous mutual aid societies, this first Jewish fraternal society was free from synagogue control, along lines similar to the Masons and other nonsectarian organizations dedicated to charitable undertakings. For a time, membership was restricted to German Jews, but later the Order accepted Jews of all backgrounds. The first meeting was held in Sinsheimer's Cafe on Essex Street, between Broome and Grand streets, on October 13, 1843, and as the organization grew, a house was purchased at 56 Orchard Street for its headquarters. By 1860 Bnai Brith boasted a nationwide membership of fifty thousand. Today it has ten times the number worldwide.

In 1846, a group of Reform Bohemian Jews organized the *Böhmischer Verein,* a cultural and social society with strong religious ties. Later that year, the group decided to establish its own congregation, and adopted the name Ahavath Chesed (Love of Kindness or Mercy). Their first place of meeting was at 69 Ludlow Street. Three years later, in 1849, they moved to 33 Ridge Street; then in 1853 to 127 Columbia Street, after which they purchased a small church at the corner of East Fourth Street and Avenue C. By 1870 many of its members had moved uptown, so the congregation decided to do the same; they engaged the well-known Jewish architect Henry Fernbach to design a new building at Lexington Avenue and East Fifty-fifth Street. A year later, the magnificent Moorish Revival-style twin-domed sandstone edifice was dedicated. Although the name Ahavath Chesed is still retained, it is officially known as Central Synagogue, and is the city's oldest Jewish house of worship in continuous use by the same congregation. In recognition of Central Synagogue's architectural beauty and historical importance, it has been designated an official landmark by the City of New York. (Actually the oldest synagogue *building* is the former Anshe Chesed, built in 1849 on Norfolk Street). The year after the opening of Central Synagogue, Congregation Shaarey Hashamayim (which had earlier voted against the plan to unite with Emanu-El) also left the Lower East Side, and in 1898 merged with Ahavath Chesed.

Other activity in the mid-nineteenth century Lower East Side includes that of a group of Dutch Jews who broke away from Bnai Jeshurun in 1847 and organized their own Congregation Bnai Israel (Sons of Israel) at 154 Pearl Street. Seven years later they rented space at 63 Chrystie Street, later moving to 41 Stanton Street. They never built a synagogue, and the congregation seems to have disappeared by 1880. The name, however, is perpetuated in a burial society.

In 1849 the Polish congregation Bikur Cholim (Visitors to the Sick) was organized at 63 Chrystie Street, possibly sharing space with Bnai Israel. Shortly thereafter they moved to 514 Pearl Street, a former courthouse, and after a brief stay, merged with the young Polish congregation, Beth Israel (see page 16). The combined congregations, unwilling to drop either name, called themselves Beth Israel Bikur Cholim, and purchased Temple Emanu-El's former Methodist Church building at 56 Chrystie Street, just across the street from where Bikur Cholim was founded.

Following the example of Ahavath Chesed and Anshe Chesed, the congregation later relocated uptown. In 1887 they moved into their new synagogue building at the corner of Lexington Avenue and East Seventy-second Street, an immense structure whose lofty twin towers dominated the neighborhood for many years. Later, the congregation shortened its name to the Park Avenue Synagogue when it erected its present neo-Romanesque style house of worship in 1926 at 50 East Eighty-seventh Street and absorbed several small congregations. Interestingly, the adjacent Milton Steinberg House, built in 1954, has a five-story stained-glass façade—the largest in the world—and was designed by artist Adolph Gottlieb.

The year Bikur Cholim was established (1849), Congregation Shaarey Rachamim (Gates of Mercy) was founded at 156 Attorney Street. Little is known about this group, except that in 1874 it purchased Anshe Chesed's famous synagogue building at 172 Norfolk Street, where it remained for twelve years. *Macoy's Guidebook to New York* for 1881 lists a Congregation Rach Mim at *146* Norfolk Street, but we know that Norfolk Street was renumbered at the turn of the century, so it is undoubtedly the same congregation; however, no synagogue records survive.

Nearby, at 63 Mott Street, which in the nineteenth century was almost exclusively a Jewish quarter but is now Chinatown, an association of Polish Jews founded Congregation Beth Avraham (House of Abraham) in 1850. Soon thereafter they moved around the corner to the old courthouse at 514 Pearl Street. An unsuccessful attempt to merge with Congregation Shaarey Zedek in its former Quaker Meeting House on Henry Street was followed by another move to 9 Henry Street. Little else is known about Beth Avraham, except that it ceased to exist after 1870.

Another Polish congregation, Beth El (House of God), departed from custom and organized "far uptown" at 1104 Broadway near Twenty-eighth Street in 1852. (This congregation is not to be confused with the Reform Temple Beth El, the successor to Anshe Chesed, which was founded in 1874. See page 21.) Four years later it rented space at 172 West Thirty-third Street, and in 1871 it merged with Shaarey Tefilah, which had just erected its new synagogue on West Forty-fourth Street two years before.

In the meantime, Congregation Bnai Jeshurun, still in its Elm Street building, found its quarters increasingly less satisfactory. Its two "errant children," Anshe Chesed and Shaarey Tefilah, now occupied elegant synagogue buildings, while its own former church structure was far too small and in need of extensive repairs. Furthermore, the once quiet, middle-class neighborhood had begun to decline. The tracks of New York and Harlem Rail Road had been pushed through to nearby Chambers Street, and although the noisome locomotives were now banned by the city fathers, the constant parade of horse-drawn trains was a continual disturbance. A site for a new synagogue was selected at 164 Greene Street, just north of Houston Street. The new building was completed in 1851 in the Gothic Revival style. It had twin towers topped by pairs of pinnacles, with a large Gothic-style rose window in the façade, above which was an ornate stepped gable. Bnai Jeshurun remained on Greene Street for only fifteen years. The neighborhood became heavily commercial, and the congregation moved to Broadway and West Thirty-fourth Street, the present site of Macy's department store. The congregation erected a rather large synagogue at Madison Avenue and East Sixty-fifth Street in 1885, and in 1918 they chose their present location at 257 West Eighty-eighth Street.

The year 1853 boded ill for three new congregations which lasted only a very short time. Neveh Zedek (Abode of Righteousness) took over Beth Avraham's meeting place at 9 Henry Street, and then disappeared from all record. Bnai Zion (Sons of Zion) was organized at 202 Houston Street, but did not last out the year. Beth Elohim (House of God), a Polish congregation at 51 Division Street and later at Number 1 on The Bowery, survived for only three or four years. It is listed in the 1857 edition of *Phelps' Guide to New York,* but nowhere else thereafter.

However, the year 1853 did mark the construction of a great, and still surviving, Lower East Side synagogue, that of Congregation Rodeph Shalom, at 8 Clinton Street. As mentioned earlier, the congregation had been meeting in a small house on Attorney Street. Their new building was constructed in an early Romanesque revival style, and is now occupied by Congregation Chasam Sopher (literally, Seal of the Scribe). The synagogue building is the second oldest in the city, and more will be said about it later. Rodeph Shalom was one of the first synagogues to adopt a moderate Reform ritual, and maintained it when they ultimately moved uptown in 1891 into Temple Beth El's building at Lexington Avenue and East 63rd Street. The congregation is now at 7 West 83rd Street.

Lest the reader get the impression that the Reform movement had completely captivated the Jewish community of New York, there remained, in addition to Shearith Israel, a number of Orthodox *shuls* (synagogues), the most important of which was Beth Hamedrash (House of Study), organized in 1852 in an attic at 83 Bayard Street. The same year, they secured rooms in a house at Elm and Canal streets, and a year later they moved to the former courthouse at 514 Pearl Street, quarters previously occupied by both Bikur Cholim and Beth Avraham. In 1856, the growing congregation bought an old Welsh chapel at 78 Allen Street, where it rapidly became the most important center for Orthodox Jewish guidance in the country.

Under Russian-trained Rabbi Abraham Joseph Ash, Congregation Beth Hamedrash pioneered in the training of Jewish scholars in America. Study as a form of religious worship was hitherto unknown in this country. Formerly, important decisions of Jewish law were rendered by the great rabbis of Europe, particularly by the Chief Rabbi of England and the Great Synagogue of London, but with the advent of Beth Hamedrash, a cadre of rabbis became available for interpretations of the law. Prior to 1840, when there were only two synagogues, the baking of matzoh and the preparation of kosher meat were under the direct supervision of the synagogues themselves. With the burgeoning Jewish population and the proliferation of houses of worship, this became virtually impossible. Yet Beth Hamedrash staunchly continued the tradition, and any *shohet* (ritual slaughterer) who received his certificate of competency from Beth Hamedrash was eagerly sought after throughout the country.

The year after the founding of Beth Hamedrash, a splinter group broke away,

25

led by matzoh baker Judah Middleman. This small assemblage of Russian–Polish Jews organized their own congregation which they called Beth Hamedrash Livne Yisroel Yelide Polen (House of Study of the Children of Israel born in Poland). Their history is not well known, but Middleman was appointed rabbi a few years later, and the group moved away from the Bayard Street house to their own *shtiebl* (small room used for prayer meetings) on Walker and Baxter streets. In 1903, their descendants reorganized the congregation, naming it The Sons of Israel Kalwarie. (Kalwarie is a small town on the Polish–Lithuanian border.) They erected their own synagogue building which still exists, and is described on page 89.

Rabbi Ash severed his ties with Beth Hamedrash in 1859, taking with him a loyal band of followers to found a rival congregation, with the competetive name of Beth Hamedrash Hagodol (Great House of Study). Converting the top floor of a private house at the corner of Grand and Forsyth streets into a place of worship, they remained there for twenty-six years. In 1885, they purchased a Baptist church at 60 Norfolk Street, and converted it into one of the most beautiful synagogues to be seen in the Lower East Side. It, too, will be discussed later. (See page 51.)

There were a number of other East Side congregations which used the name Beth Hamedrash, but none seems to have survived for any great length of time. *Lloyd's Guide Through New-York City* for 1866–1867 lists a Beth Hamedrash Second at 157 Chatham Street (now Park Row), while Hyman B. Grinstein, in his monumental *Rise of the Jewish Community of New York,* speaks of the existence of several *batai medrash* ("houses of study") in addition to Beth Hamedrash and Beth Hamedrash Hagodol.

Another Orthodox congregation, Shaarey Beracha (Gates of Blessing), was founded by French Jews from Alsace in 1858. They held their first services in a house on Attorney Street and then moved to a number of different locations in the Lower East Side. In 1890, they moved to East Forty-seventh Street between Second and Third avenues; then in 1894, to a site on East Fiftieth Street. Shaarey Beracha subsequently purchased the Adas Israel (Community of Israel) Synagogue on East Fifty-seventh Street and remained there until 1909, having merged with Temple Israel. Other than these frequent changes of address, little substantive information is known about this congregation.

Completing the picture of the major synagogues established prior to the era of mass immigration are three congregations not organized on the Lower East Side. The first, Aderet El (Glory of God), was organized by a group of German Jews in 1859 on East Twenty-third Street near Third Avenue. The congregation no longer exists, although one with a similar name on East Twenty-ninth Street was founded in Harlem at the turn of the century. The second was Emunath Israel (Faith of Israel), founded in 1865 on West Eighteenth Street. After a move to West Twenty-ninth Street, it settled in 1920 at its present site at 236 West Twenty-third Street, acquiring the building of the defunct Third Reformed Presbyterian Church. The third, Congregation Darech Amuno (The Way of Faith), was dedicated in the early 1860s at 53 Charles Street in Greenwich Village, and its present building on the site dates from 1903.

THE ERA OF MASS IMMIGRATION

The masses of immigrants who came to the "City of Promise" in the small waves of 1836 and 1848 were relatively minor compared with the tidal waves which swept our shores from eastern Europe without cease from 1880 to World War I, and again from 1919 to 1924. Almost two million Jews came to America, most of them settling for a time in the Lower East Side. In the two-square-mile corner of Manhattan bounded by the East River and The Bowery and by Catherine Street and East Fourteenth Street, they crowded into block after block of dismal tenements, creating the world's largest ghetto. By the turn of the century, the population density of the Lower East Side rose to an astonishing 986 inhabitants per acre, which was one-and-a-half times as many as there were in Bombay, India.

After enduring the ordeal of a long and arduous passage in the steerage of cramped, foul ships, the immigrants were then crowded into equally miserable living quarters—buildings hastily constructed by speculators, without comfort or convenience, which soon became synonymous with grinding poverty and a squalid existence. Few came with skills adaptable to the New World, except for peddling and manual trades such as tailoring, baking, shoemaking, cigarette making, or butchering. Consequently, most were sucked into the home sweatshop industry of the garment trades or became small shopkeepers or pushcart peddlers.

The reasons for the sudden huge migration from eastern Europe were many—famines, epidemics, the threat of military conscription, periodic pogroms, and a general economic decline throughout Europe—all in addition to the severe restrictions against Jews. In 1868, a cholera epidemic swept the steppes of Poland and Russia. A year later, famine starved out tens of thousands. In 1871, a pogrom, inspired by the Czar, sent many fleeing westward. After the assassination of Czar Alexander II in 1881, new and even more restrictive laws were promulgated against the Jews, which forced them to abandon their rural villages and move to towns and large cities. Barred from all professions and the opportunity to receive a higher education, Jews were driven to engage in petty handicrafts, operate small businesses, or become merchants. And so they came to America—the *Goldeneh Medina* (Golden Land), hoping for a new life.

Most immigrant Jews from eastern Europe had been living in the Pale of Settlement, a broad region originally established by King Boleslav of Poland in the thirteenth century to attract Jews who might further the economic growth of the area. The Pale extended from the Black Sea almost to the Baltic, and included much of the Ukraine, Byelorussia, Lithuania, Poland, and eastern Rumania. Jews made up a significant percentage of the population of such cities as Warsaw, Bialystok, Cracow, Vilna, Lwow (Lemberg), Kovno, Minsk, Odessa, Poltava, Kishinev, and Jassy.

In Russia, the Kishinev pogrom of 1903, the Russo–Japanese War of 1904–1905, the abortive revolution of 1905, and a succession of government-sanctioned pogroms forced thousands to flee. In the year 1905 alone, over one hundred thousand sought refuge in America. Just a few short years later, New York had the largest Jewish population of any city in the world.

As the east European Jews jammed into the Lower East Side, the established, middle-class German Jews departed in haste. What had begun in the 1860s as a slow movement uptown to the "nicer neighborhoods" soon became a mass exodus. The remaining German Protestants also fled, mostly to Yorkville. The social and cultural gap between the established Jews and the new arrivals became an ever-widening breach. The German Jews regarded with contempt the ways of the poorer "Galitsianers" and "Litvaks"—their earthy habits and mannerisms, their strange dress and folkways, the lack of education and small town or *shtetl* mentality, their "medieval" orthodoxy, and their exclusive use of the Yiddish language which the Germans regarded as only a jargon. The east European Jews, in turn, thought of the Americanized Jews as haughty and indifferent, and regarded those who had adopted Reform Judaism as virtual *goyim* (Gentiles). The wide economic and social differences, as well as the growing geographical separation, divided them into what would later be referred to as the "Uptown" and the "Downtown" Jews.

There were other differences between the east European Jews and their Americanized Orthodox brethren. Perhaps the most significant was the newly arrived Jews' concept of *kehillah,* or community. Things had changed greatly since Colonial days when Shearith Israel was the only congregation in New York, when there was in effect a close-knit community, with laws that governed not only the religious ritual, but to an extent the daily life of each member. Although the Sephardim were Orthodox and very observant of religious laws, they were also worldly and tended to mingle socially and commercially with their non-Jewish neighbors. The assimilation process was hastened with the arrival of the Ashkenazic German-speaking Jews in the nineteenth century and the spread of the Jewish community throughout the city. With the establishment of synagogues far from each other in different neighborhoods, and the somewhat diminished leadership role of the rabbi, community control by the synagogue had virtually broken down. The Jews who arrived before 1880 had not gathered in ghettos but had integrated quickly into the American society. The synagogue for them was no longer the center of daily life, but only of religious ritual.

The Jews arriving from eastern Europe, however, could not adjust to such a nontraditionalist way of life. They were much more rigorist and fundamentalist and firmly rooted in a community structure which they were loath to relinquish. In the Pale of Settlement, czarist edicts had forced the Jews into a state of virtual political, economic, and cultural isolation, with each *shtetl* (town) having its own well-organized *kehillah* (community). At its head was the rabbi, who was responsible for the welfare of the community and who served as its teacher, judge, interpreter of the law, and performer of civil ceremonies, such as weddings. As mentioned earlier, his role as a leader of the ritual was less important, since every adult male in the community was assumed to be equally well trained. If the town could afford one, there was a *hazzan* (cantor, among the east European Jews), a *shohet* (ritual slaughterer), a *mohel* (circumcisor), and in the larger towns, a *bes din* (religious court), and a *dayan* (judge). The community also maintained a *mikveh* (ritual bath), a *cheder* (religious school), a *hekdesh* (communal room used as a hostel for poor travelers), a *gemilas chesed* (charitable society), a *bikur cholim* (visitors to the sick), a *bes olam* (burial ground), and a *chevra kadisha* (society which takes care of funeral and burial arrangements).

Within the east European immigrant community, Yiddish was the only form of communication. Hebrew was spoken by the more learned, used only for prayers (which all could read), and was considered a sacred language. In addition, many Hebrew words and expressions appear in the Yiddish language. The regional languages of the Pale (Russian, Polish, Lithuanian, Hungarian, Rumanian, etc.) were used only in dealings with the outside world.

After the immigrants were admitted to the United States at Castle Garden Immigration Station and later at Ellis Island, these tightly knit Orthodox groups settled among their countrymen on the Lower East Side. They sought to live and work near each other and maintain most of their traditions undisturbed. They tended to gather by regions of origin within the crowded neighborhood, establishing mini-communities of *landsleit* (fellow countrymen) in what were called *chavarot* * (mutual benefit societies). As the term is used today, a *chevra* is a small congregation of members from the same region. In rented attics, basements, storefronts, and apartments, these *chavarot* proliferated on every block on the Lower East Side.

The rapid growth of these societies led to the formation of an institution almost unique to the East Side, the *landsmanshaft* (literally, a society of fellow countrymen). These secular organizations, usually named after their members' home towns in Europe–Odesser Verein, Suwalkier Society, Bialystoker Center– were founded on principles of self-help rather than of charity, and functioned primarily as social and mutual benefit societies, generally without religious activities. Among the many valuable services which the *landsmanshaft* provided to its members were financial aid, *bikur cholim* (visits to the sick), and *chevra kadisha* (funeral and burial arrangements). The purchase of a cemetery plot would be one of the first concerns of the society.

It was in the meeting room of the *landsmanshaft* that the men would gather for an exchange of ideas and information, for news of employment opportunities, to talk over old times, drink a glass of tea, read letters from loved ones in Europe, or discuss politics and current events. Women, too, were often active in the social activities of the society, and would proudly refer to themselves as being "society ladies." Just after the turn of the century it was estimated that there were well over half a million members and at least three thousand *landsmanshaftn.* Today only one such organization survives, the Bialystoker Center and Bikur Cholim at 228 East Broadway. Interestingly, it was also the first *landsmanshaft* to be established in America.

The various enclaves of the Lower East Side developed characters of their own, as the Galicians (from eastern Austria–Hungary and western Poland) settled south

---

* Although such Hebrew words as *chavarot* and *yeshivot* are the plural forms of *chevra* and *yeshiva,* the Ashkenazic Jews from eastern Europe pronounced the final *-ot* as *es,* and would transcribe it that way in Yiddish; likewise, such words as *beth* and *adath* were written and pronounced *bes* and *adas.* Words of Germanic origin generally followed their own rules for the plural; however, such Yiddish diminutives as *shtetl* and *shtiebl* used the old Judeo-German plural, *shtetlach* and *shtieblach.*

of Delancey Street; the Rumanians, along Chrystie and Allen streets between Houston and Grand streets; the Hungarians, north of Houston Street and east of Avenue B; the Lithuanians, along Monroe, Madison, and Grand streets; and the Levantine Jews (from Syria, Turkey, Palestine, Iraq, and the Balkans) elbowing in among the Rumanians. However, the great influx of Russian Jews in 1905 broke down the demarcation lines to a great extent as they moved in wherever they could find space in the congested neighborhood. The names inscribed on many of the surviving synagogue buildings reflect the geographic distribution of these immigrants; for example, First Roumanian–American Congregation, Bialystoker Synagogue, Erste Warshawer Congregation, and Makower of Poland.

It is estimated that between 1880 and 1915 more than five hundred Jewish houses of worship were organized in the Lower East Side. In an actual count taken in the year 1905, there were three hundred fifty congregations functioning. In all, about sixty buildings were built expressly as synagogues, including about a dozen converted churches. The other places of worship were rebuilt private dwellings, meeting halls, or, most commonly, *shtieblach* (literally, small rooms). The *shtiebl* could be a remodeled living room, an attic, a basement, or an entire apartment of a multiple dwelling house which was used by one or more *chavarot* exclusively for religious services. In addition, there were *talmudai torah* (religious schools), 335 in the year 1905, and countless *chedarim* (one-room after-school Bible and Hebrew classes for young boys). Several *yeshivot* (religious seminaries) were founded, among which were the Rabbi Isaac Elchanan Theological Seminary and the Yeshiva Etz Chaim (Tree of Life). The two later merged and moved uptown to become Yeshiva University. The only surviving yeshiva in the Lower East Side, and possibly the most influential in the Orthodox community in America, is the Mesifta Tifereth Yerushelaim (Seminary of the Glory of Jerusalem) at 145 East Broadway, whose spiritual leader, Moshe Feinstein, is universally recognized as America's leading Hebraic authority.

The rise of the Lower East Side Jewish community in the great era of immigration is a phenomenon unequalled in history. Cherishing a religious heritage nurtured in the *shtetlach* (towns) of eastern Europe, these poor Jews struggled to build a new life in the unfriendly, teeming streets of New York. Against the backdrop of a daily life of misery in the comfortless tenements, the back-breaking drudgery of the sweat shops, fairly widespread anti-Semitism, and an unending fight for survival, a new and vital culture emerged, which changed not only the destiny of the immigrant, but also that of the land to which they had brought their faith, ideals, and dreams. For many, the Lower East Side became the portal to America and the stepping-stone to a new and better life. Out of these endless hardships arose a rekindled spirit, a reawakening which stimulated intellectual and artistic creativity. The Yiddish language achieved a new status which was reflected in a rich and varied literature, a vibrant and compelling theater, a wealth of published books, and a profusion of daily and weekly newspapers. Tens of thousands of copies were sold of the works of Isaac Peretz, Mendele Moicher S'forim, and Sholom Aleichem. And the stages of the Yiddish rialto, first on the Bowery, Grand and Houston streets, and later along Second Avenue, echoed to the resounding lines of Jacob Adler, Maurice Schwartz, Sigmund Mogalesco, David Kessler, and Boris Thomashefsky.

The lively and influential Yiddish press, personified by Abraham Cahan's socialistically oriented *Forward,* was particularly responsible for the rapid adaptation of the "greenhorns" to the complex life in America. The *Forward* championed the poor working man and fought indefatigably for better labor conditions; and its still popular column, *A Bintel Brief* (literally, Bundle of Letters), printed the editor's solutions to many of the personal problems of its immigrant readers. But not everyone read the *Forward,* for its political convictions and frequent irreligious attitude were resented by some. There were other dailies which competed with the *Forward,* at least six at the turn of the century, among which the most popular were the *Tageblatt,* the *Morning Journal,* and the *Day.*

The Lower East Side, with all its oppressiveness and suffering—or perhaps because of it—became the arena for a Jewish renaissance, attracting intellectuals from around the world and providing the environment for social change. So many, whose careers began in the ghetto will never be forgotten—Irving Berlin, Eddie Cantor, Edward G. Robinson, Jan Peerce, Felix Frankfurter, Meyer London, David Dubinsky, to mention but a few. From the East Side came the impetus for the rise of the labor movement and the birth of such unions as the United Hebrew Trades and later the Amalgamated Clothing Workers and the International Ladies Garment Workers Union. Change, however, came slowly and painfully, at the cost of countless strikes, political battles, infighting among rival labor groups, and the loss of 146 young garment workers in the dread Triangle Shirtwaist Company fire.

Other institutions, too, had their genesis in the Lower East Side. The Workmen's Circle *(Arbeiter Ring)* was founded in 1892 as an outgrowth of the *landsmanshaft* movement. A socialist fraternal organization, it provided medical care and burial benefits, and offered the immigrants a secular Jewish education through lectures and classes.

The Educational Alliance, still serving the East Side community on its original site at East Broadway and Jefferson Street, was organized in 1889 by a group of philanthropic uptown Jews as an educational, cultural, intellectual, and service center for the residents of the Lower East Side. It took over the work of the Hebrew Free Schools Association and offered children's classes in Jewish religion and history. Its landmark Americanization Program, supported by funds from the Baron de Hirsch Fund, provided day classes for newly arrived immigrant children to prepare them for entry into the public schools. The Alliance's day and evening classes in English and citizenship for adults were used as a model by New York City's Board of Education for their own later programs. (Today, it is the Board that provides the English teachers at the Alliance for a new immigrant constituency.) The Educational Alliance was a pioneer in the field of summer camping, sending undernourished poor youngsters for a few weeks to the country. It also established The Legal Aid and Desertion Bureau to assist the Yiddish-speaking immigrants with their myriad problems in the new homeland.

In 1893 a young German–Jewish nurse from an uptown middle-class background was called on an errand of mercy to the Lower East Side. Appalled at the health and sanitary conditions she saw in the tenements, Lillian Wald made the decision of her life, to help the afflicted. She moved into a cold-water flat around the corner from the Educational Alliance at 27 Jefferson Street, and with the financial support of banker and philanthropist Jacob Schiff she founded the Nurses' Settlement. She later moved to larger quarters at 265 Henry Street, and changed the name to the Henry Street Settlement. As the Settlement grew, Miss Wald persuaded the city to organize a public nursing program and also to place nurses in the schools. She fought vehemently against the abuses of child labor and stood beside the striking cloakmakers in their bitter struggle against subhuman working conditions. The Henry Street Settlement has expanded its programs greatly through the years and still performs a vital service to the community.

An even older social agency is the University Settlement Society, at Rivington and Eldridge streets. Functioning in many ways similar to both the Henry Street Settlement and the Educational Alliance, it provided much needed help to the surrounding immigrant community—and still does to this day, although the clientele is no longer only Jewish, but Spanish and other nationality groups.

The single most important institution to the immigrant Jews, however, was the *shul,* or synagogue. While not everyone was a passionate follower of the traditional Orthodox rituals, the *shul* was the center for most immigrants of Jewish life. It

33

was their visible reminder of God and the place where they could commune with Him. And to them, the synagogue was tangible evidence of the continued existence of their old-world Jewish traditions.

While many of the synagogues were simply converted tenement apartments, a surprising number of splendid houses of worship were erected, a few of which still remain. Although most of the immigrants arrived in this country with little more than the clothes on their back, they managed to pool their meager resources, borrow where they could, and erect dozens of imposing synagogues. Some of these buildings were former Protestant churches which they acquired and remodeled, much as did their early nineteenth-century Ashkenazic predecessors. Some more fortunate *chavarot* were able to purchase the synagogues of German–Jewish congregations that were moving uptown—fleeing the "onslaught" of the masses of east European Jews. Today only a small number of these synagogues survive.

DECLINE OF THE LOWER EAST SIDE

The Jewish population of the Lower East Side is now but a fraction of what it was in its heyday seventy-five years ago, with no more than twenty-five thousand remaining, representing a mere thirty percent of the total neighborhood population. Most live in small enclaves of the once sprawling ghetto; and had it not been for the construction of the post-World War II cooperative apartment houses along Grand Street and the East River, there would likely not be a single active congregation left.

The highpoint of immigration into the Lower East Side was reached around 1905, but not all remained. For more than a decade, a small but steady exodus had been taking place to Harlem, and by World War I, that neighborhood was almost exclusively Jewish. While there was a constant influx of newcomers from Europe to take their place in the East Side, a second east-European quarter began mushrooming in the Brownsville section of Brooklyn, and in just a few years there were no less than seventy synagogues erected in that fast-growing area that had been farmland in the 1890s. With the opening of the Williamsburg Bridge in 1903, thousands of tenement dwellers suddenly seemed to discover other parts of Brooklyn, and within a few years, Jews made up a significant percentage of the population of such sections as Boro Park, Williamsburg, and East New York.

34

After World War I, other Jews settled in Washington Heights, Flatbush, Crown Heights, and along the Bronx's Grand Concourse. The highly restrictive immigration law of 1924 effectively put an end to any further influx from eastern Europe, and the population of the Lower East Side began a rapid decline. By the 1930's the first synagogue abandonments took place. One of the first to close its doors was the great Mishkan Israel Suwalki Synagogue at 27 Forsyth Street. The building, erected in 1901, was sold to St. Barbara's Greek Orthodox Church, and it is still there, near the Manhattan Bridge exit, its large twin domes and Byzantine façade reminiscent of the days when it was one of the most prominent Jewish landmarks in the neighborhood. Ironically, the Suwalki congregation also had its beginnings in a church. The congregation, organized in 1886, first met in the former Methodist church on Chrystie Street which had been used by Temple Emanu-El and Beth Israel Bikur Cholim.

Dramatic evidence of the gradual shrinking of the Lower East Side Jewish community can be seen in the former Anshe Tifereth Jerushelaim synagogue at 87 Eldridge Street, sold in the early 1960s to a Black Methodist congregation. The building still retains the *Mogen David* symbols and Hebrew lettering on its façade. A more recent, and more shocking abandonment was that of the popular Congregation Anshe Ileya at the corner of Forsyth and Delancey streets. Known to all East Siders as the Forsyth Street Shul, it had had the reputation for being well-endowed and well-attended, and its sale to a Dominican Seventh Day Adventist church startled and saddened the community. A lesser, but still quite visible synagogue closing was that of the Independent Kletzker Brotherly Aid Society on Ludlow Street, just north of Canal Street. The building, erected in 1892 by a *chevra* from Kletzk, Poland, served also as a mutual benefit organization, and after it closed, it was purchased by a funeral parlor, which uses the old sanctuary for its own purposes and rents out the rest of the building as artists' lofts and apartments.

One by one, the *shuls* have been deserted or left to the care of small congregations of mostly elderly members. Many have closed their elaborate sanctuaries, using the basement *bes medrash* (literally, house of study) for services, if and when a *minyan,* or quorum of ten adult males, can be assembled. And the surrounding neighborhood, once almost exclusively Jewish, is now becoming foreign and frequently hostile; on dark winter evenings, many old people must be escorted by police to their Sabbath services.

But the spirit still lives on, particularly in the small group of remaining synagogues, nurtured by the handfuls of *landsleit* who come faithfully, week after week, replacing a smashed window pane, installing a new door lock, repairing a broken fixture, or just trying to keep ahead of the destructive effects of weather and vandals. And as true *landsleit* they would never think of merging their group with another small *chevra,* preferring instead to maintain their own identity, even at the risk of losing the *shul.* And what of the dwindling cadre of dedicated rabbis, some whose miniscule congregations can no longer afford to pay them a salary? They too live on, working as best they can, remembering the glorious past, and hoping in vain for the future.

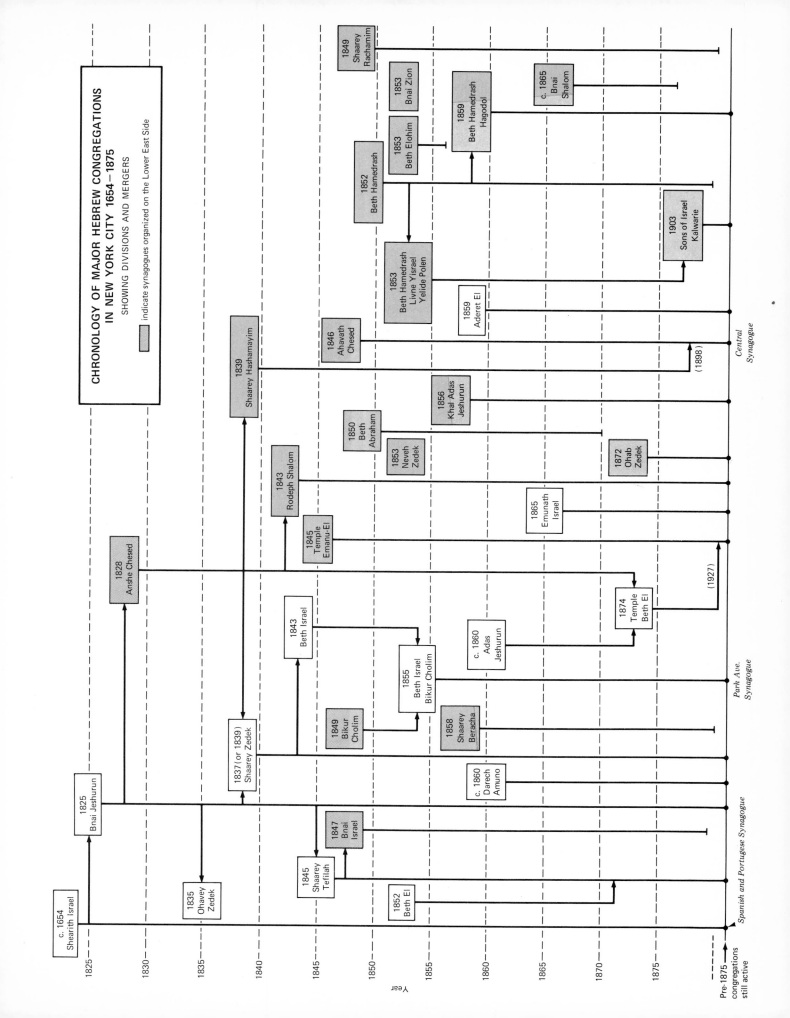

CHRONOLOGY OF MAJOR HEBREW CONGREGATIONS
IN NEW YORK CITY 1654–1875

SHOWING DIVISIONS AND MERGERS

indicate synagogues organized on the Lower East Side

Congregations mentioned in Part One:

Page:

Adas Jeshurun (1860?-1874) — 20
Aderet El (1859-   ) — 26
Ahavath Chesed (1846-   ) *Now, Central Syngogue* — 16
Anshe Chesed (1828-1874) — 14
Beth Avraham (1850-1870?) — 24
Beth El (1852-1871) — 24
Beth Elohim (1853-1857) — 24
Beth Hamedrash (1852-1875?) — 25
Beth Hamedrash Hagodol (1859-   ) — 26
Beth Hamedrash Livne Yisroel Yelide Polen (1853-1903) — 26
Beth Israel (1843-1855) — 16
Beth Israel Bikur Cholim (1855-   ) *Now, Park Avenue Synagogue* — 23
Bikur Cholim (1849-1855) — 23
Bnai Israel (1847-1880?) — 23
Bnai Jeshurun (1825-   ) — 11
Bnai Zion (1853) — 24
Darech Amuno (1860?-   ) — 27
Emunath Israel (1865-   ) — 27
Neveh Zedek (1853) — 24
Ohavey Zedek (1835) — 14
Rodeph Shalom (1843-   ) — 16
Shaarey Beracha (1858-1900?) — 26
Shaarey Hashamayim (1839-1898) — 15
Shaarey Rachamim (1849-1886) — 23
Shaarey Tefilah (1845-   ) — 16
Shaarey Zedek (1837?-   ) — 14
Shearith Israel (1654-   ) — 7
Temple Beth El (1874-1927) — 21
Temple Emanu-El (1845-   ) — 19

PART TWO

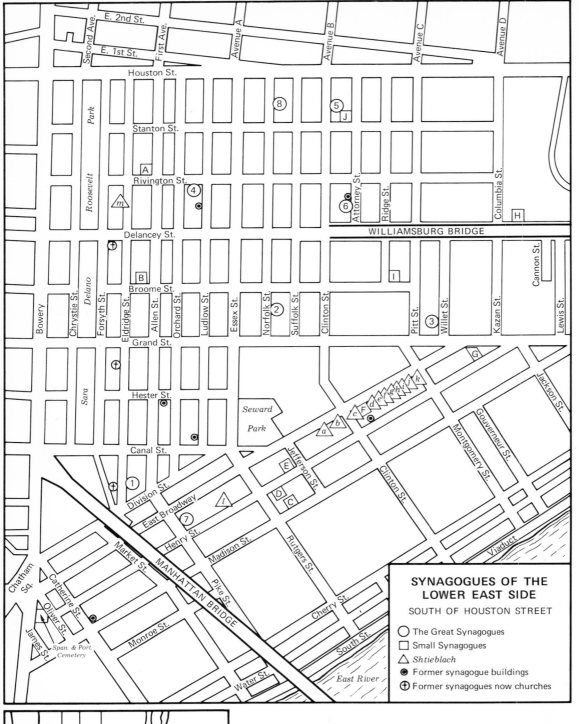

SYNAGOGUES OF THE LOWER EAST SIDE
SOUTH OF HOUSTON STREET

○ The Great Synagogues
□ Small Synagogues
△ *Shtieblach*
◉ Former synagogue buildings
⊕ Former synagogues now churches

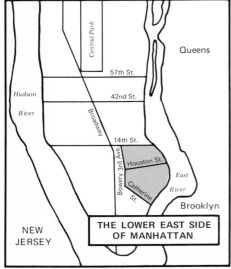

**THE LOWER EAST SIDE
OF MANHATTAN**

THE GREAT SYNAGOGUES

(Numbers correspond to location on map)

1. Congregation Khal Adas Jeshurun with Anshe Lubz, 14 Eldridge Street
2. Beth Hamedrash Hagodol, 60 Norfolk Street
3. Bialystoker Synagogue, 7 Willett Street
4. First Roumanian-American Congregation, 89 Rivington Street
5. Congregation Chasam Sopher, 8 Clinton Street
6. Beth Haknesseth Mogen Avraham, 87 Attorney Street
7. Congregation Sons of Israel Kalwarie, 15 Pike Street *(abandoned 1977)*
8. Congregation Anshe Slonim, 172 Norfolk Street *(abandoned 1974)*

THE GREAT SYNAGOGUES

The synagogues described in the following section are in the southern part of the Lower East Side, below Houston Street. The synagogues are identified by numbers or letters and the location of each is indicated by the identifying number or letter on the map on the facing page.

A visit to the sanctuaries of the synagogues of the Lower East Side is like a trip into the past. Three of them are over one hundred years old, and while most try to keep up appearances, little has changed inside or out since the synagogues were built. Sitting in quiet contemplation in these cavernous and ornate halls, one can easily conjure up the scene of seventy-five years ago, when the great halls and galleries were filled to overflowing, and undulating masses of *talith*-draped worshipers stood swaying in a cacaphony of devotions led by the plaintive chant of the *hazzan* proclaiming the glory of God.

It was customary for the larger synagogues to have two rooms for worship, an upstairs main sanctuary, called in Yiddish the *aybershter* (upper) *shul,* and the downstairs *untershter* (lower) *shul,* often called the *bes medrash* (house of study). Weekday services were conducted in the lower *shul,* while the more heavily attended Sabbath and holy day services were held in the main sanctuary. Overflow crowds on the High Holy Days were usually accommodated at separate services downstairs. The demand for seats at Rosh Hashanah and Yom Kippur was so great that space was often rented in public halls, theaters, and movie houses. The lower *shul* was also used for weddings, important functions, and social events.

41

1. Khal Adas Jeshurun with Anshe Lubz
(Community of the People of Israel with the People of Lubz)
14 Eldridge Street

Congregation Khal Adas Jeshurun was founded in 1856 by a group of Polish Jews, thirty years before the construction of this magnificent building. By 1872, the congregation had grown sufficiently to engage its first full-time rabbi, Isaac Gellis. Unfortunately, Rabbi Gellis is remembered more today for the delicatessen factory he established on Essex Street, than for his work as spiritual leader of the congregation. Perhaps his moment of greatest pride came in 1887 when the new synagogue building was dedicated. It was designed by the noted architectural firm of Herter Brothers and became the first synagogue to be erected on the Lower East Side by the east-European Jews. It was also the largest in the neighborhood and retains that distinction to this day. Shortly after the dedication of the new building, a Polish *chevra* (small congregation) called Anshe Lubz merged with the congregation, adding its name to the title.

The building is an interesting combination of Moorish, Gothic, and Romanesque elements, and the façade appears in virtual pristine condition. Only the parapet with its ornamental finials is missing. Most striking are the typically Moorish keyhole-shaped doorways and window openings. Entry is gained now through the side door—the main doors at the top of the broad staircase have been sealed for many years—to the basement *bes medrash* (house of study). Here Sabbath and daily *mincha* (afternoon) services are conducted if a *minyan* (quorum) can be assembled. The room is a miniature synagogue, with a central *bimah* (reader's platform), carved wooden Ark (cabinet to store the Torah scrolls), *ner tamid* (eternal light) suspended above the Ark, rows of benches, and a separate section for women behind a wooden screen to the rear. In the corridor leading from the street is a wall safe which once served as a collection box for contributions, with the purpose of each donation indicated in Hebrew above the various slots (for the Hebrew school, prayer books, etc.).

The real attraction is the upstairs sanctuary, abandoned since the early 1930s. It is reached by passing through a small vestibule, whose rolled sheet-tin walls and ceiling are badly rusted, and climbing a creaky wooden staircase up to the main lobby, which is strewn with shards of smashed stained glass, chunks of fallen plaster, and the accumulated dust of over forty years. A leaking roof has allowed rain and snow to wreak havoc, and the rotting staircases leading to the women's gallery above seem in imminent danger of collapse. Only a half-light filters through the remaining stained glass windows—the electricity has long ago been shut off above the basement.

Opening the glass doors to the sanctuary is an awesome experience, however, for little has changed through the years. Immense brass chandeliers with Victorian glass shades hang from the seventy-foot ceiling. Once lit by gas, they must have flooded the immense room with an aura of soft light. The *bimah,* or reader's platform, is located in the center of the hall, with four brass torchères at each corner, also adorned with Victorian glass. A brass crown motif appears on all lamp fixtures, and their conversion to electricity was done inconspicuously, although the old gas lines are still visible along the walls. The huge Ark, carved in Italy of walnut, dominates the front of the sanctuary. Behind its sliding doors are kept a number of old Torah scrolls to supplement those used downstairs. Fading trompe l'oeil paintings, barely visible on the cracking plaster, adorn the walls to the right and left. Above, the brass *ner tamid* (eternal light), with its crown design, hangs unlit. The spacious gallery is also faced with walnut, the back rows disappearing into the semidarkness.

Looking up and to the rear, one can see narrow rays of light streaming in through the immense stained-glass wheel window, while on the surrounding wall, brightly painted gold stars still shine brightly on a dark blue background. At each front corner hang small wooden cabinets containing *megillot* (scrolls) of various books of the Bible. A feeling of great height is created by the barrel-vaulted ceiling with rows of miniature domes supported by graceful columns. Prayer books are strewn about in disarray on the dusty Gothic-style benches. Most of them were printed in Vilna, Lithuania, in the first decade of the twentieth century, and they show the effects of years of use and the destructive dampness of the old building. And scattered about the sanctuary floor are a number of colorful ceramic spitoons.

In the front lobby are marble memorial plaques with the names of mostly forgotten congregants, except for Rabbi Isaac Gellis and Sender Yarmulovsky. The latter's ill-fated private bank on Canal Street collapsed in 1914, taking with it the lifelong savings of many Lower East Siders and the treasury of the nearby Beth Hamedrash Hagodol synagogue. The congregation, now numbering fewer than twenty active members, can barely support its rabbi, Samuel S. Gringras, who conducts daily *mincha* (afternoon) and *maariv* (evening) services whenever a *minyan* can be assembled.

Although there has been some movement to preserve and protect this magnificent building, little has so far been accomplished. The Jewish Museum has shown interest in having the sanctuary converted into a synagogue museum;

however, extensive rehabilitation and restoration must be undertaken first at considerable cost. So, until some organizations or private donors come forth to rescue it, the future of this great synagogue remains uncertain.

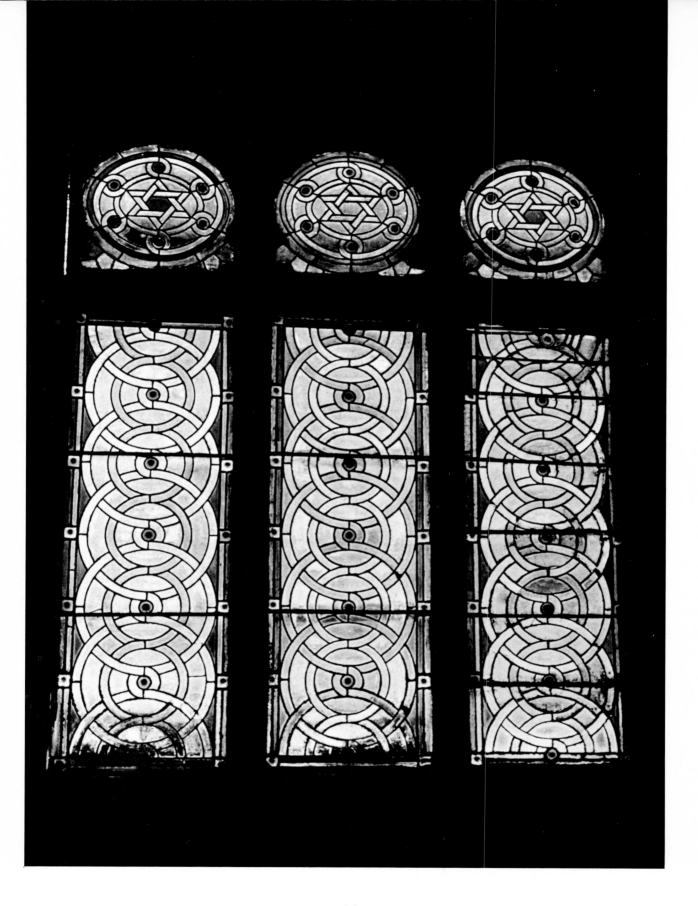

46

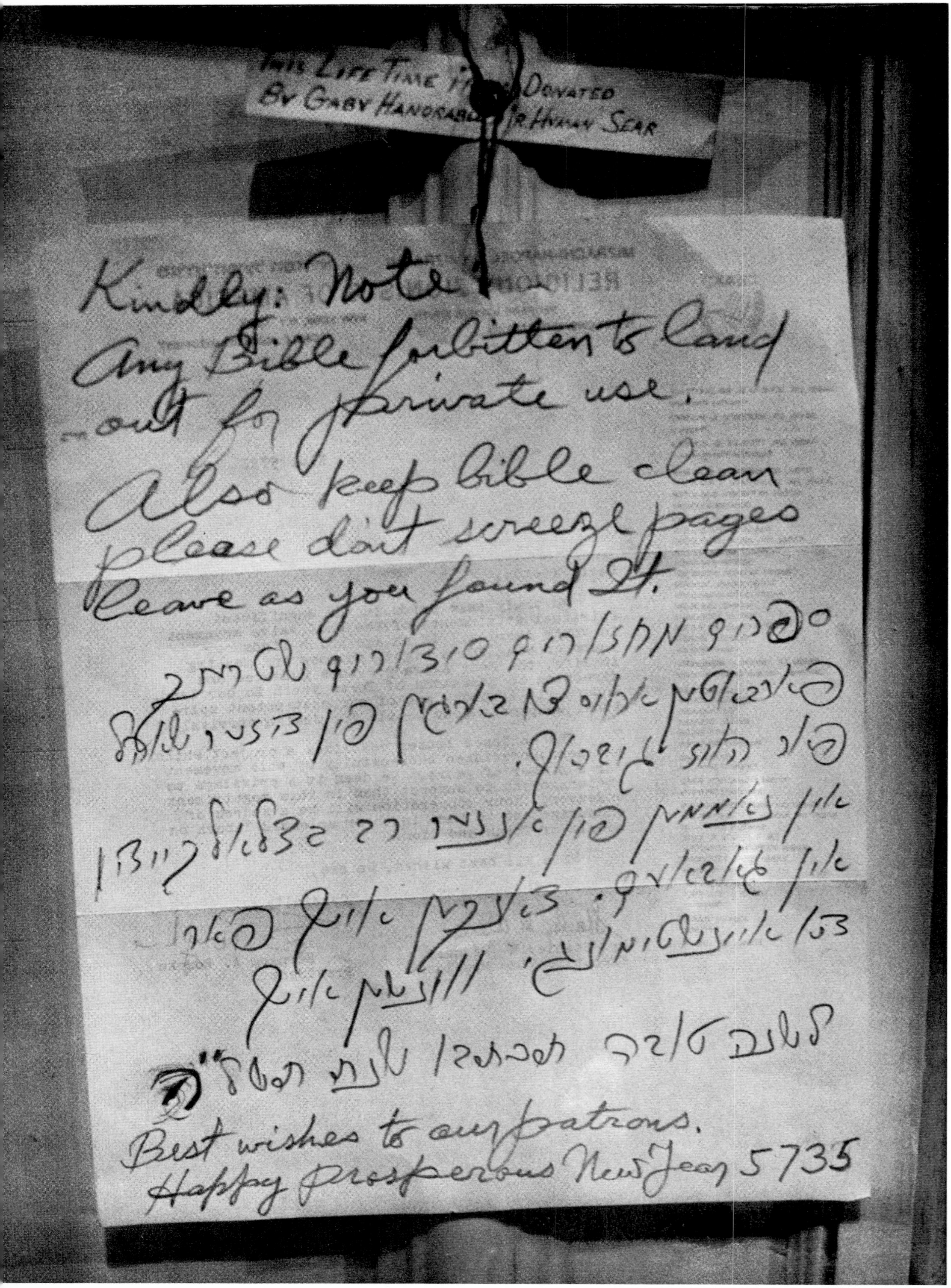
Kindly: Note
Any Bible forbitten to land
out for private use.
Also keep bible clean
please don't screezl pages
leave as you found It.
Best wishes to our patrons.
Happy prosperous New Year 5735

BETH HAMEDRASH HAGODOL

2. Beth Hamedrash Hagodol
(Great House of Study)
60 Norfolk Street

This congregation, an outgrowth of the original Beth Hamedrash, founded by Rabbi Abraham Joseph Ash in 1852, is the oldest Orthodox Ashkenazic house of worship in New York City. It was also the first Russian–Jewish Orthodox *shul* in the country and enjoyed the reputation of being an important center of religious learning for Jewish scholars. The synagogue is open daily and conducts several *minyanim.*

In 1885 the congregation purchased the building from the Norfolk Street Baptist Church and moved from their former quarters in the old Welsh chapel on Allen Street. The structure is a twin-tower Gothic-Revival-style building, with much of the former ornamentation removed. A bright new coat of paint has transformed the old dull exterior into a proud showplace for this historic synagogue. The sanctuary is singularly beautiful. Many of the old church furnishings still remain—the carved pews, ornate gallery, and typical Gothic vaulted ceiling. The Ark occupies the place of the former church's pulpit, and the building walls have been repainted with colorful Biblical scenes. The *bimah* in the center of the hall is surmounted by four charming globe-shaped lamps of etched glass. In the late afternoon, sunshine streaming through the stained glass windows fills the broad sanctuary with a myriad of colors. The building, which dates from the mid-nineteenth century, is well maintained and remains in a good state of preservation. Beth Hamedrash Hagodol is one of two Lower East Side synagogues to be designated an official New York City landmark (the other is the Bialystoker Synagogue).

The first and only chief rabbi of the Orthodox Jewish community, Rabbi Jacob Joseph, became rabbi of Beth Hamedrash Hagodol in 1899. He had been brought to New York from Vilna eleven years before by the Association of American Hebrew Orthodox Congregations; but the multifaceted Lower East Side religious community was not willing to support a "chief" rabbi, nor was the good rabbi equal to coping with the internecine quarrels among such organizations as the complex kosher-meat industry. He was, however, a most pious and respected community leader and founded the largest Jewish secondary school on the East Side, which bears his name to this day. At his death in 1902, the Jewish community turned out en masse for his funeral, and a procession estimated at twenty-five thousand marched from synagogue to synagogue in one of the city's greatest solemn marches. No other "chief" rabbi has ever been appointed.

The present rabbi is Ephraim Oshry, president of the Rabbinical Board of New York and president of the Rabbis Survivors from Concentration Camps. He is an outstanding scholar and author. During the Nazi occupation of his native Lithuania, Rabbi Oshry lived in the Kovno ghetto, helping survivors maintain the quality of Jewish life despite the agonizing oppression. After the war he opened a yeshiva in Rome, and later served as a rabbi in Montreal. On the hundredth anniversary of the founding of Beth Hamedrash he was appointed spiritual leader of the congregation, and at the same time published a historical novel on the terror in his homeland—*The Ruins of Lithuania.* In his four-volume *Teshuvot Mi-Maamakim* ("Responsa from the Depths"), Rabbi Oshry provides a compilation of answers to questions asked by Jews about to enter the gas chambers. Two other works, *Imrei Ephraim* and *Divrei Ephraim* offer an interpretation of the laws of Jewish daily life for those about to face death. The rabbi emphasizes that "Jews should know not only the gruesome facts about the extermination of our brothers and sisters, but also the story of the heroic battles in the ghettos."

By keeping the synagogue open every day and maintaining a charity fund for those in need as well as for religious education, Rabbi Oshry adheres to the age-old traditions of the European synagogues which stressed "prayers, Torah, and charity." He sees Beth Hamedrash Hagodol recreating the role of *shul* in the "old country" which cared for the poor who huddled on the synagogue steps and which served as a center for religious learning and inspiration.

56

THE BIALYSTOKER SYNAGOGUE

3. The Bialystoker Synagogue
   7 Willett Street

In 1878, the congregation of Beth Haknesseth Anshe Bialystok (Synagogue of the People of Bialystok) was organized in rented quarters in a tenement at 48 Orchard Street. (Bialystok, a city and province in Russia, and later, Poland, had one of the largest Jewish populations in the Pale of Settlement. The city's bakers are credited with the invention of that very popular onion roll, the *bialy).*

The congregation purchased the Willett Street Methodist Episcopal Church in 1905. The building, which dates back to 1826 when the area was semirural, is a very solid, austere Federal-style structure unlike any other in the neighborhood. It is described by the New York City Landmarks Preservation Commission as "a building of rugged simplicity and straightforward honesty in design and construction." The exterior is of fieldstone and is topped by a peaked roof, with no tower or steeple—an excellent example of the type of building construction of our nation's early period. The synagogue was designated an official landmark in 1972.

The interior is surprisingly bright and decorative. The fine stained-glass windows cast brilliant rays of red and blue across the rows of oak pews. The ceiling is decorated with the signs of the zodiac and the Hebrew months. One wonders, incidentally, why the painter chose a *trayf* (non-kosher) lobster as one of the symbols. On the front wall are paintings by a local artist depicting the Mount of Olives and a fanciful conception of King Solomon's Temple. The most imposing feature is the Ark, which is almost three stories high. The three large crowns represent the *Keser Torah* (Crown of the Torah, or Law), the *Keser Malchus* (Crown of the Kingdom of Israel), and the *Keser Cahuna* (Crown of the Priesthood).

The Bialystoker Synagogue is still very active and has, perhaps, the best attendance on the Lower East Side. It is maintained in excellent condition, supported mainly by congregants living in the adjacent Sidney Hillman Houses. Services are held four times each morning, as well as *mincha* (afternoon) and *maariv* (evening) prayers. Cantors are considered a rare luxury these days, and recently the Bialystoker Synagogue was fortunate in having a visiting *hazzan* from Kiev. The spiritual leader, Rabbi Irving Singer, has served the synagogue for many years and is an influential member of the Lower East Side community.

61

FIRST ROUMANIAN-AMERICAN CONGREGATION, SHAAREY SHAMOYIM

4. First Roumanian–American Congregation, Shaarey Shamoyim
(Gates of Heaven)
89 Rivington Street

The origin of this Rumanian congregation is somewhat obscure. Records show that a *chevra* with the same Hebrew name and calling itself The First Roumanian Synagogue, was organized in 1860 at 70 Hester Street. In an 1866 city guidebook it is listed at 91 Rivington Street, adjacent to the address of the present congregation. This Shaarey Shamoyim congregation should not be confused with the much older German group founded in 1839, Shaarey Hashamayim, whose name translates the same.

The *pinkas* (minute book of the synagogue) does show that in 1885 the congregation was reorganized and added the word "American" to its name. By about 1890 they acquired the Memorial Methodist Church which had formerly been located around the corner at 126 Allen Street and had in 1888 erected a new church at the present site at 89 Rivington Street. Why they built such an enormous building for a dwindling congregation is a mystery.

After remodeling the church building, the Rumanian congregation converted the adjacent rectory into a *Talmud Torah* (Bible school), which still functions today. The synagogue retains virtually all the exterior ornamentation of the former church, which is reminiscent of a medieval castle and the only example of the Romanesque Revival style in the area. By contrast, the interior is rather elaborate. The sanctuary, which is entered on the second floor, is extremely wide, with a huge gallery extending halfway down the hall, following the pitch of the sloping floor. The seating capacity exceeds sixteen hundred, making it one of the largest synagogues in the city. The *bimah,* or reader's platform, is set very close to the pulpit, rather than in the more customary central location. The building faces south, which contributes to the cheerfulness of the hall, and the artistic stained-glass windows add to the pleasant illumination. The Ark is delicately carved and situated beneath the broad windows. There is a large *bes medrash* (literally, "house of study," where daily services are held) on the lower floor, and rather extensive facilities for social events.

The congregation is considerably smaller than it was even a few years ago but is still very active, especially the busy ladies' auxiliary. However, it is no longer Rumanian. The Rumanian Jews, avowedly fun loving, enjoyed singing, dancing, dining, and drinking, and every cantor had in his repertoire that popular folk tune

Rumainye! Rumainye! Most of the present membership is drawn from among the merchants of nearby Orchard and Essex streets.

An interesting aspect of the *shul*'s history is that it was a mecca for great cantors. In the heyday of the Lower East Side, no *hazzan*'s reputation had been firmly established until he had chanted the prayers at the Roumanian Synagogue. Among the larger Lower East Side *shuls,* the intense competition and bitter rivalry to obtain the cantorial talents of the big-name *hazzanim* sometimes reached scandalous proportions. In that era it was the treasured ambition of every young boy with a good voice to become a *hazzan.* Since the sale of seats for the High Holy Days was their chief source of income, *shuls* fortunate enough to engage the talents of Pinkhas Minkovsky, Israel Cooper, Zavl Kwartin, or Yossele Rosenblatt could be assured of redeeming their debts and having a year of financial stability. The fervent adoration of East Siders for brilliant cantors was like that of opera lovers for their favorite stars. Cantors such as Sirota, Vigoda, Hershman, Katchko, and Roitman intoxicated worshipers with their individualistic chanting of the inspiring hymns. Their unique trills and free vocalization, which gave their own sweet melodic interpretation to the liturgical chants, elevated cantorial music to new heights in the United States.

It was here at the Roumanian *Shul* that the career of the great Moishe Oysher was launched, as well as that of Jacob Pincus Perelmuth, better known as Jan Peerce. It was Peerce who offered the *shul* a free concert if they would allow his brother-in-law, a budding cantor, to sing. The congregation reluctantly agreed, and young Richard Tucker was on his way to his own successful singing career. Yossele Rosenblatt, the greatest cantor of them all, sang for a time at the Roumanian *Shul* before joining the Ohab Zedek congregation in Harlem. But the Roumanian synagogue's greatest contribution to the world of Jewish cantorial music was made when it brought European *hazzan* Moishe Koussevitzky to the *shul* to begin a long, star-studded singing career.

The congregation's present rabbi, Dr. Mordecai Mayer, who was ordained in Lublin, Poland, at the age of 19, came to America in 1940 and served as rabbi of the Chasam Sopher Synagogue (see page 69). Twenty years later, he left Chasam Sopher and became the spiritual leader of the Rumanian *Shul*. Rabbi Mayer is proud of the fact that his congregation maintains one of the last surviving synagogue-connected *Talmud Torahs* on the Lower East Side. He has firmly resisted efforts to modernize the operations of the synagogue: "We don't want to change our beloved *Rumaynishe Shul* and sacrifice our dignity." Declining many invitations to serve congregations elsewhere, Dr. Mayer feels that he belongs to the Lower East Side, "among the simple, good-hearted people–those closest to God."

CONGREGATION CHASAM SOPHER

5. Congregation Chasam Sopher
8 Clinton Street

Congregation Chasam Sopher occupies the second oldest synagogue building in New York, built for the German–Jewish Congregation Rodeph Shalom in 1853. Designed in the novel *rundbogenstil,* or round-arch Romanesque Revival style, the synagogue was a close rival to its three-year-old neighbor, Anshe Chesed, two blocks away on Norfolk Street.

The red brick synagogue building has undergone many exterior modifications since its construction. A grand staircase leading from the street to the second-floor sanctuary is no longer used, nor are the doorways at street level opening to the women's gallery staircases. The castellated parapet on its two square towers is gone, as is the original Ark in the sanctuary. The hall is surprisingly large, devoid of ornamentation, painted a bright white, and topped with a high barrel-vaulted ceiling. The gallery is supported by clusters of thin colonnettes, which add further to the feeling of spaciousness. The present Ark, of carved oak, is a clever re-creation, on a small scale, of the front façade of the building with all the round-arch Romanesque Revival details.

When Congregation Rodeph Shalom moved out, there was no shortage of new east-European congregations to take over the building. Three years before, two small Polish *chavarot* (congregations) named after their home towns, the *shtetls* of Czestochowa and Unterstanestier, merged to form Congregation Chasam Sopher. The literal meaning, Seal of the Scribe, refers to Moshe Schreiber (1762–1839). He was also called by his un-Germanicized name, Moshe Sofer, since he was a descendant of a series of Torah scribes, or *soferim.* Moshe Schreiber was born in Frankfurt and became a highly respected rabbi and talmudic scholar known particularly for the simplicity and clarity of his lectures and for the more than one hundred manuscript volumes left after his death. He traveled widely throughout Austria–Hungary, founding *yeshivot* and benevolent institutions in several cities. He later gave up the rabbinate and settled in Pressburg where he founded the famous Pressburg Yeshiva. When the Reform movement was initiated in Hamburg in 1819, he dedicated his life to fighting against it with all his strength. It must therefore have seemed like poetic justice to the new congregation named for Rabbi Moses Schreiber to displace a Reform group and take over their synagogue.

The congregation's membership today is much too small to support a rabbi, but daily *minyanim* are conducted nonetheless. Since the immediate surrounding neighborhood is no longer Jewish, the small but fiercely dedicated remaining members struggle bravely to keep the *shul* going. Much credit must be given to the congregation's president, Moses Weiser, and to his son Eugene who serves without compensation as the *shammos* (sexton). As with so many congregations, they survive through the loyalty and efforts of a handful of members. The idea of a merger with another synagogue, while ostensibly a practical solution to the problem of dwindling membership, is anathema to them, despite the historic mergers of former years. Their zeal in protecting the identity of their own synagogue has indeed proved costly, since a marginal existence is the most that these small congregations can expect.

CONGREGATION BETH HAKNESSETH MOGEN AVRAHAM

6. Congregation Beth Haknesseth Mogen Avraham
(Synagogue of the Shield of Abraham)
87 Attorney Street

This building was erected by the First Protestant Methodist Church in a modified Greek Revival style, about 1845. The Protestant Methodist sect did not last very long and subsequently sold the church to a Black congregation, which renamed it the Emmanuel African Methodist Episcopal Church. A Polish group, calling itself the Erste Galitsianer Chevra (First Galician Congregation), purchased the church in 1884 and later adopted the name Mogen Avraham. Remodeled as a synagogue, it has been in continuous use by them ever since, although the name was changed shortly after the turn of the century. To adapt the former church sanctuary to synagogue use, a *bimah* was installed in the center, the walls and ceiling were repainted with zodiac symbols and scenes of the Holy Land, and the *Mogen David* (Star of David) was set into the stained-glass windows above the small gallery. The *bimah* is quite attractive with its decorative lamps and ornamental brass scrollwork. Structurally, the building is most interesting as a period piece with its rolled sheet-tin walls and ceilings, narrow winding wooden staircase, gas-fired radiators, and outside plumbing. Being somewhat smaller than most of the great Lower East Side synagogues, its sanctuary and downstairs *bes medrash* have a rather warm, intimate quality. Friday evening services in the shadowy, dimly-lit basement, with the sparse assemblage of bearded and solemn *talith*-draped worshipers quietly reciting their devotions, evoke a sombre old-world atmosphere.

The synagogue boasts an active membership of about seventy-five, mostly drawn from the nearby co-ops along Grand Street and the East River. Rabbi Elias S. Heftler has served the tightly knit congregation for over twenty years and is staunchly dedicated to preserving a vital Jewish community on the Lower East Side, which he refers to as "the cradle of Judaism in the United States." Mogen Avraham has weekly *minyanim* in the *bes medrash* and conducts holy-day services in its well-maintained sanctuary.

The small red-brick house just north of the synagogue was built originally as the parsonage for the former Emmanuel A. M. E. Church. It later served as the *shammos'* house when the Erste Galitsianer Chevra acquired the church next door. In recent times, the aging little house belonged to a small *chevra* called the Rozwadwer Synagogue and Landsmanshaft, and their name in Yiddish letters is barely discernible on the wooden sign which brackets the entrance. There is a *bes medrash* on the first floor, but the upper stories are vacant.

88

CONGREGATION SONS OF ISRAEL KALWARIE

7. Congregation Sons of Israel Kalwarie
15 Pike Street

The *Kalvarier Shul* is the newest of the great synagogues, built in 1903. It is named for the village on the Polish–Lithuanian border from which most of its congregants came during the period of the great immigration. The congregation itself is older, and dates from 1853, when a number of Polish and Russian members broke away from Congregation Beth Hamedrash. In 1899, the congregation, which had adopted the ungainly name of Beth Hamedrash Livne Yisroel Yelide Polen (House of Study of the Children of Israel born in Poland), merged with the newly arrived Polish *chevra* from Kalwarie, and settled upon the present name.

The impressive classic-style building rises above a high basement, on both sides of which are twin lateral stairways leading to the columned portico of the main entrance. The sanctuary, now in a sad state of disrepair, is nevertheless awe inspiring. The front wall is faced with travertine, as is the very elaborate Ark. Standing just in front is a large, leaf-scroll brass Menorah. Similar candelabra adorn the central *bimah*. Thick imitation marble columns support the rear gallery, above which are broad stained-glass windows. Colorful clerestory windows beneath the ceiling add illumination to an otherwise sombre interior. This is the only East Side synagogue with seat cushions on its benches, but they are soaked with dampness and rotting away. The scene in the sanctuary is now one of decay and neglect. Broken glass from vandals' missiles litters the floor, and large flecks of faded paint drop from the peeling walls and ceiling. Many Menorahs and all brass adornments have been pilfered by intruders. The congregation has not had a rabbi for a number of years, but services were occasionally held when a *minyan* could be gathered in the downstairs *bes medrash;* however, at this writing it appears that the synagogue has been abandoned entirely.

In its days of glory after the turn of the century, the *Kalvarier Shul* was the East Side's favorite synagogue for large ceremonies and affairs. It was the site on January 10, 1913 of a near riot when more than five thousand young people tried to force their way into the building to hear the first in a series of Friday night religious lectures by noted rabbi Judah L. Magnes. The rabbi had just broken with Reform Judaism, resigned his post at Temple Emanu-El, and joined the Orthodox Movement. So great was the pressing crowd attempting to gain entrance to the *Kalvarier Shul*'s sanctuary that a squadron of mounted police had to be summoned; they maintained control only with the greatest difficulty, and the iron fence which once stood in front of the *shul* was bent to the ground. The reason for all this tumult (discussed in the section on small synagogues under the description of the Young Israel Synagogue) was the excitement at the birth of the Orthodox Young Israel Movement, which took place that night at the *Kalvarier Shul.*

With the disappearance of the congregation, the future of the synagogue building is in grave danger. Unless the building is protected, it will soon fall victim to greater vandalism and weather damage, and maybe even worse.

CONGREGATION ANSHE SLONIM

8. Congregation Anshe Slonim
(People of Slonim)
172 Norfolk Street

It is hard to believe that this crumbling, decrepit building, now abandoned to vandals and the elements, was once the city's largest and most influential synagogue. The history of the former Anshe Chesed congregation is related at some length in Part I. When the synagogue building was completed in 1850, it was the largest in the United States, seating seven hundred on the main floor and five hundred in the gallery. It was also the third congregation to be organized in New York (after Shearith Israel and Bnai Jeshurun) and the first to embrace the Reform movement. Today, it is the oldest surviving synagogue building in New York, and probably the third oldest in the country.

When Anshe Chesed moved uptown in 1874 (see page 23), the building was purchased by Congregation Shaarey Rachamim (or Rach Mim) which stayed for twelve years and then vanished. The venerable synagogue was then acquired by Congregation Ohab Zedek, popularly called the First Hungarian Congregation, and for twenty years it was the spiritual and cultural center of the large number of Hungarian Jews who had settled in that section of the Lower East Side. In 1906, Ohab Zedek moved to a thriving new Jewish neighborhood in Harlem, and the building stood vacant for a number of years, except for its basement *mikveh* (ritual bath) which was maintained by an adjoining Russian-Turkish bath establishment.

In 1921 a *chevra* of Polish Jews from the town of Slonim (now a part of Byelorussia) took over the unoccupied building. The congregation remained active until early 1975 under the leadership of Rabbi Max Kohn, but a rapidly dwindling membership, abetted by continual harassment of the small *chevra* by new and hostile neighbors, forced them to abandon the synagogue.

The building was designed by Jewish architect Alexander Saeltzer in the then popular Gothic Revival style. Saeltzer's other major work, erected simultaneously, was John Jacob Astor's library, which later became the headquarters of the Hebrew Immigrant Aid and Sheltering Society (HIAS) and is now the New York Shakespeare Festival Public Theater. It is said that the architect was influenced by the occasion of the impending completion of Germany's Cologne Cathedral, and adopted the general plan of the Cathedral's exterior to this synagogue. The twin towers of the structure were once capped by ornate octagonal pyramids. Three large Gothic-style windows on the first and second stories are framed by narrow lancet windows in the towers. Quatrefoil designs appear in the arches and in the two tiny windows in the gable. Unfortunately, most of the ornamentation has been stripped away, the windows have been sealed, and the stuccoed brickwork is hidden under layers of peeling and faded pink paint. A small stone plaque above and to the left of the main doorway is weatherworn and barely legible and gives some of the later history of the synagogue.

The vast interior, now a total shambles, still shows some evidence of its original graceful Gothic-style design, with a high vaulted ceiling, clustered supporting columns, trefoil and quatrefoil motifs in the gallery railing, and an enormous rose window with colored glass panels representing the Ten Commandments. The Ark has been smashed and its splintered doors hang limply on broken hinges; shreds of prayer books and ripped Torah cases have been strewn about the debris-littered floor; benches and lamp standards have been overturned; metal fixtures (including the plumbing) have been stripped; and pigeons fly in and out of the empty windows to perch on the gallery railing above. The wretched scene of desolation and desecration is shocking and disheartening.

The future of this historic synagogue is in serious jeopardy. To rescue it from its present status as an unsafe building with a court order for demolition pending, requires immediate action by some interested group willing to protect it and find some appropriate adaptive reuse. Otherwise, public apathy will condemn this famous landmark to the wrecker's ball.

SMALL SYNAGOGUES SOUTH OF HOUSTON STREET

The small synagogues of the Lower East Side are divided into two groups in this book—those located south of Houston Street in what is now the heart of the East Side, and those north of Houston Street to East Fourteenth Street, in what is popularly called the East Village. The synagogues in the south section can be located on the Lower East Side map on page 40, those in the north section, on a separate map on page 142. Should one wish to make a tour of these synagogues, one can follow the alphabetical sequence on the main map and the numerical sequence on the second map, and the complete circuit can be made without having to double back or retrace one's steps. Space does not permit a lengthy account of all the small synagogues, therefore only those of special religious, historic, or architectural interest are described.

(Letters correspond to location on map on page 40)

A. Erste Warshawer Congregation, 60 Rivington Street *(abandoned)*
B. Congregation Kehila Kadosha Janina, 280 Broome Street
C. Beth Haknesseth Etz Chaim Anshe Wolozin, 209 Madison Street
D. House of Sages, 152 Henry Street
E. Congregation Senier and Wilno, 203 Henry Street *(burned out)*
F. Young Israel Synagogue of Manhattan, 225 East Broadway
G. East Side Torah Center, 312 Henry Street
H. Erste Litowisker Chevra, 292 Delancey Street
I. Downtown Talmud Torah Synagogue, 142 Broome Street
J. Congregation Bnai Jacob Anshe Brzezan, 180 Stanton Street

A. Erste Warshawer Congregation
(First Warsaw Congregation)
60 Rivington Street

This is the most imposing of the small synagogues, and was erected by this Polish congregation from Warsaw in 1913. The broad façade is vaguely Byzantine in character, and the suggestion of twin towers gives the impression of even greater size. Sadly, much of the exterior ornamentation has been stripped away over the years, and the exposed brickwork creates a scarred effect. The oversize circular window is particularly attractive, set in its round frame of Hebrew letters with the name of the congregation in bold relief. The large central doorway beneath opens directly from the sidewalk to a staircase leading up to a wide vestibule, where both side walls are covered with ornate marble memorial plaques.

The interior is an unexpected delight. This is the only East Side *shul* whose sanctuary has *two* galleries! Looking up from the floor of the hall, the effect produced by the extremely wide overhang of the lower gallery is one of being at the bottom of a deep chasm. The effect is heightened when one climbs to the rear of the upper gallery, from which point only the central *bimah,* the Ark, and a very narrow section of benches can be seen on the sanctuary floor, and even they are partially obscured by several enormous bronze chandeliers suspended on long chains below the level of the galleries. One can only speculate on the vivid and stirring tableau of fifty years ago, with the brilliantly lit hall and galleries packed with High Holy Day worshipers, and the rabbi and *hazzan* in their religious white raiment leading the clamorous congregation in prayer. Who in that animated scene of long ago could have envisioned this dusty and silent hall of today?

Until the recent demise of Rabbi Nuta Shainberg, the *Warshawer Shul* maintained Sabbath services in its basement *bes medrash.* Now, however, there is no longer a congregation, and the building stands vacant, its doors barricaded against vandals by a group of dedicated volunteers based at the Educational Alliance who are called the Synagogue Rescue Project and who seek to recover and preserve the religious artifacts of abandoned synagogues before they are stolen and the buildings demolished.

108

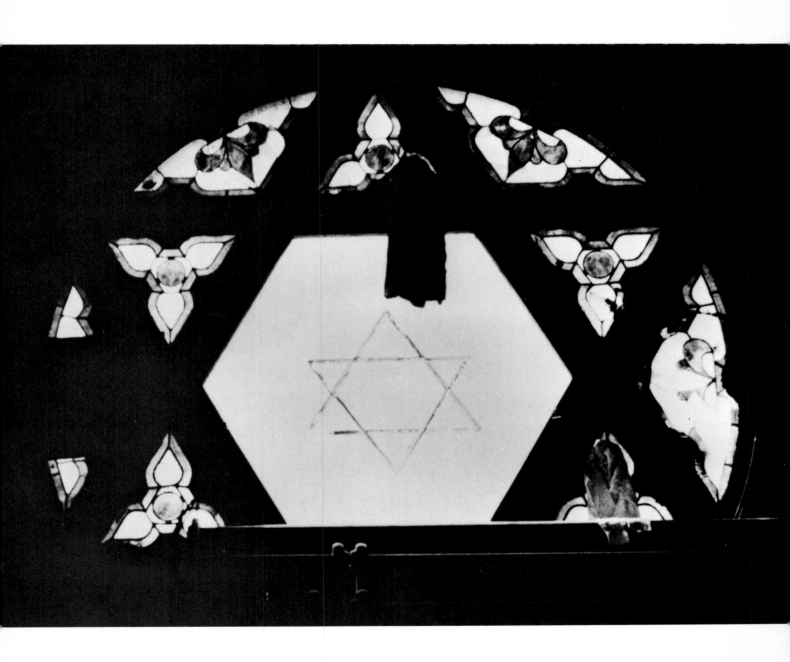

B. Congregation Kehillah Kadosha Janina
(Congregation of the Holy Community of Janina)
280 Broome Street

One of two remaining Sephardic congregations on the Lower East Side, the *Janiner Shul* is named for the city which once had the largest Jewish population in Greece. The congregation was organized in 1906 at the start of the influx of Levantine Jews, but the synagogue was not built until 1927. Although very few *Sephardim* still live in the neighborhood, enough worshipers come to Saturday morning services to keep the little *shul* functioning. The spiritual leader is Rabbi Morris Cassulo.

C. Beth Haknesseth Etz Chaim Anshe Wolozin
(Synagogue of the Tree of Life, People of Wolozin)
209 Madison Street

Almost hidden between two tenement buildings, this small brick synagogue, built in the early 1890s by a *chevra* from Wolozin, Poland, still hangs on, although it is now in a virtually alien area. Madison Street was one of the first to be settled by immigrant Jews as early as 1825. This *shul,* however, was erected when the Lower East Side became a haven for tens of thousands of Jews from eastern Europe. Note the unusual *kiddush*-cup motif over the doorway as well as other ornate terra cotta designs above the stained glass windows. What was once a circular glass window has been boarded up and decorated with a large *Mogen David.*

D. Agudas Anshei Mamod Ubeis Vead Lachachomim
(House of Sages)
152 Henry Street

Unlike the other synagogues which function for an outside congregation, the House of Sages conducts daily services for a resident group of retired rabbis (and for anyone else who may wish to attend). Although they do not live on the premises, these elderly sages call this their home, coming daily to pray, meet friends, talk over old times, discourse on points of talmudic law, recite *yizkor* (memorial) prayers for those wishing them, or just relax among their contemporaries. The building is relatively new, erected in 1940, and the institution is supported by voluntary contributions. Dr. Julius G. Neumann, the director and vice-president, is an active community leader.

E. Congregation Senier and Wilno
203 Henry Street

Only the burned-out shell remains of this once proud and active synagogue. It fell victim to arson in late 1975, and its once lovely interior was completely destroyed.

The *shul* was built in 1893 and called Makower of Poland. Later it became the Wilno (from Vilna, Lithuania) *Shul,* and after the burning of the *Sineerer Shul* at Madison and Montgomery Streets in 1972, that congregation merged with this Wilno group, only to have their synagogue burned out again. The former house of worship was also used by a small Hasidic *chevra,* Tifereth Achim Sfard Anshe Polen.

It appears that the former Makower congregation went to great lengths to convert a mid-19th century multiple dwelling house into what at first glance looks like a building erected expressly as a synagogue. The destruction of this venerable *shul* shocked and outraged the community. Now marked for early demolition, the totally gutted synagogue with its smashed stained glass windows, fire-scarred dome and *Mogen David,* and ruined interior stands as a sad reminder of the ever-present sickness of anti-Semitism.

F. Young Israel Synagogue of Manhattan
225 East Broadway

The synagogue building, a converted apartment house, is more significant in its mission than in its appearance. Young Israel purchased the house in 1921 from the Hebrew Immigrant Aid and Sheltering Society when the HIAS moved uptown (see page 96) and converted it to the headquarters of this movement of young Orthodox Jews which has branches throughout the world. The movement was founded in 1912 when the Lower East Side was the bastion of Orthodoxy and the center of Jewish intellectual life in America. Many of the young Orthodox Jews viewed with alarm the growing popularity of the Reform movement, the spread of antireligious socialism, and the rise of crime among Jews.

The organization had its genesis in an event which took place one Friday evening at Clinton Hall on Astor Place, in the upper reaches of the Lower East Side. Much interest had been generated by the speeches of the famous Zionist leader and Reform rabbi, Stephen S. Wise, and when it was announced that he would deliver a lecture on Judaism, many Orthodox youths, eager to hear the rabbi, packed the hall. In the course of the evening, baskets were passed around for a collection. The young people, astonished and outraged at this violation of Sabbath laws which forbid the handling of money, even for charitable purposes, hooted disapproval, threw buttons into the baskets, and stalked out in anger. They then sought out Benjamin Koeningsberg, a local attorney and civic leader, and together with a number of Orthodox friends, went to call on one of the great Jewish community leaders, Dr. Judah L. Magnes, to discuss what seemed to them a direct threat against the Jewish religion, and what action might be taken. The outcome was a series of lectures by Dr. Magnes given at the *Kalvarier Shul* on religious themes to help counter what they considered blasphemy. The excitement of the opening night lecture was heightened by one of the largest demonstrations in the history of the Lower East Side.

The young Orthodox Jews came enthusiastically to the series of lectures which was continued for many years. It was during one of his presentations that Dr. Magnes suggested that this movement should have an appropriate name, and when someone cried out, "We in America are the young of Israel!" he responded excitedly, "Yes, yes, that shall be the name, 'Young Israel.' "

The activities of Young Israel in promoting Orthodox Jewish living for young people extend to many areas—college campuses, resident and day camps, literary groups, and the many youth programs sponsored by Orthodox congregations.

Women now participate equally, no longer screened out by a curtain, as in the *Kalvarier Shul* back in 1913. Rabbi Sherman Siff is the religious leader and advisor of this Young Israel center.

G. East Side Torah Center
313 Henry Street

The Center is located in a pair of early 19th century Greek Revival-style residences which extend through to Grand Street, and many of the c.1830 architectural details still remain, particularly the arched entranceway with keystone block and the panelled lintels over the windows. The institution which dates from the turn of the century also shares space with a small *chevra,* called the Slutzker Synagogue (from the town of Slutzk, Poland), the diminutive Yeshiva Konvitz, and Talmud Torah Rabbi Jacob David. The combined Center, under the direction of Rabbi Seymour Nulman, serves a constituency in the nearby co-ops and low-income housing projects; the rabbi is recognized as a distinguished Lower East Side community leader.

H. Erste Lutowisker Chevra
(First Lithuanian Congregation)
292 Delancey Street

This synagogue, in the shadow of the Williamsburg Bridge, is commonly called the Lithuanian *Shul*. Many of the congregants in the nearby housing projects are from, or are descendants of immigrants from, Lithuania. During the Middle Ages, Lithuania was one of the largest and most influential states in eastern Europe, and its capital, Vilna, remained such an important center of Jewish culture that Napoleon once called it "The Jerusalem of Lithuania." One of the member groups of the *shul* is the Society of Young Talmudists. The single-story red brick building was dedicated in 1965 as the Lutowisker Congregation Machzike Hadass.

I. Downtown Talmud Torah Synagogue
142 Broome Street

When this institution was organized in the mid-1890s on Houston Street, it boasted more than seven hundred full-time students. In 1959, when the center erected the present building close to the mushrooming co-ops, it still had an active religious school for young men; but with the rapidly dwindling constituency of recent times, the Talmud Torah was forced to cease operations. The Synagogue does, however, maintain the small Beth Jacob Yeshiva for Girls, and the attractive synagogue sanctuary is used by the neighboring community on the Sabbath. Rabbi Aaron Kahn is proud of the hundred or so boys and girls who come regularly on Saturday mornings to *daven* (pray). Often, pre-*bar-mitzvah*-age boys are allowed to *daven* alongside the adults as encouragement to further religious study and a possible cantorial career. The Synagogue claims the distinction of having the youngest age group of any Lower East Side *shul.*

CONGREGATION BNAI JACOB ANSHE BRZEZAN

J. Congregation Bnai Jacob Anshe Brzezan
(Congregation Sons of Jacob, People of Brzezan)
180 Stanton Street

Named for a small town in Poland, this house of worship was erected in 1910. The immediate neighborhood, once almost exclusively Jewish, has declined considerably, and the congregation is now very small. The *shul*'s survival is attributable mainly to its very energetic rabbi, Joseph Singer (a cousin of Rabbi Irving Singer of the Bialystoker Synagogue), who keeps his dwindling flock together with daily morning prayers. The diminutive synagogue is barely twenty feet wide, but the sanctuary measures 110 feet from the entrance to the Ark. The hall is charming in its simplicity, with rough benches, a plain reader's platform, an unadorned wooden Ark, primitive wall paintings of the Hebrew month motifs, a rolled sheet-tin ceiling, and gas-fired radiators. Above the Ark is a large panel with a pair of hand-painted lions. The downstairs *bes medrash* is intimate and even more simple. The pews are shiny oak benches from mid-nineteenth century public school classrooms, and still have their traditional inkwell holes. The women's gallery upstairs is also furnished with rows of old, second-hand school desks.

SHTIEBLACH

Shtiebl is the Yiddish word for "small room" *(shtieblach* in the plural). The term is applied to those very small *chavarot,* or congregations, located in tenement apartments, storefronts, or even basements and attics. They are almost invariably composed of fellow countrymen from the same east European town or village, and are generally either too small or too poor to have their own synagogue building.

Most of the *shtieblach* are found in the two blocks of East Broadway between Jefferson and Montgomery streets, many sharing the same premises. One may indeed wonder why there is the need for so many mini-congregations when there are still a number of large and small synagogues scattered throughout the Lower East Side. The answer lies in the custom of self-segregation by *shtetl,* or town of origin, which took hold the moment the immigrants arrived, and is rooted in the tradition of the self-contained societies in eastern Europe. No one knows for sure how many *shtieblach* existed at the height of the immigration period, but estimates place the number at well over five hundred, with one or more on every block.

For years, East Broadway has been considered the citadel of Orthodoxy in America. To this day it is dotted with many Orthodox landmarks, from the Mesifta Tifereth Yerushelaim yeshiva, the long row of still-active *shtieblach,* the Young Israel Synagogue, the Bialystoker Center, to the last surviving public *mikveh* on the Lower East Side, at the intersection of Grand Street.

In the heyday of the Lower East Side, less religious Jews referred to the two-block stretch of East Broadway between Clinton and Rutgers street as the Athens of the Lower East Side. In that short distance were the Educational Alliance, three Yiddish dailies (the *Tageblatt, Morgen Journal,* and the *Forward),* the new Seward Park Library, and several book stores and publishers.

Many of the *shtieblach* belong to Hasidic groups. The *Hasidim* have lived on the Lower East Side in small numbers since the first waves of east European immigration, but after World War II large numbers came from Poland, Hungary, and Rumania. Most settled in the Williamsburg, Crown Heights, and Boro Park sections of Brooklyn, but some joined their brethren on the East Side. They dress distinctively and maintain a distance from other Orthodox Jewish groups, mingling only when necessary. Modern Hasidism—*hasid* means "pious one" in Hebrew—was founded in eighteenth-century Poland by Israel ben Eliezer, who was called by his followers *Baal Shem Tov* (Master of the Good Name). The movement began as a reaction to the overly academic and inflexible attitudes of Jewish religious leaders at the time. In essence, the hasidic spirit is characterized by an intense concentration during the performance of religious acts and an unbounded joy in devotion. The Hasidim believe in direct communion with God and great emotional exaltation in prayer. They assert that one must enjoy one's relationship with the Almighty, and thus they sing, sway, and often dance during prayers; and they live by a rigorously interpreted set of talmudic laws. Although considered extremists by fellow Jews who do not accept their fundamentalist philosophies, dress, and separatist attitudes toward worldliness and women, the Hasidic movement has been gaining steadily in popularity, particularly among young people.

The Hasidim can be easily distinguished by their obviously distinctive manner of dress. Hasidic men wear beards, *payot* (side curls), dark broad-brimmed hats, and *kapote* (long black coats). Young boys wear the *payot* and a *yarmulke* (skull cap). Hasidic women dress fairly conventionally but never have their arms exposed, and their dresses are always high-necked. After marriage, they shave their heads and wear the *shaitel,* or ritual wig. There are various classes of Hasidim, based on social rank, and these range from *modernish* (modern) to *zehr Hasidish* (very Hasidic), each with distinctive features of clothing. The highest rank are the *rebbes* who wear a broad sable hat called a *shtreiml;* a long dark, silky coat with pockets in the back, known as a *bekecher;* plus white knee socks, *zocken,* into which their breeches are tucked; and *shich,* which are slipper-like shoes.

The two major Hasidic groups in New York are the Lubavitchers from Poland, who follow Rabbi Menachem M. Schneerson of Crown Heights, and the Satmar Hasidim, who migrated from Rumania to Hungary and came to the United States after World War II. The Satmar *rebbe* is Rabbi Joel Teitelbaum of Williamsburg.

Only one Sephardic *shtiebl* exists on the Lower East Side, Congregation Ahavath Shalom Monastir (Love of Peace of Monastir), at 133 Eldridge Street. This group dates from a second Sephardic immigration which took place between 1908 and 1914, particularly in 1912 and 1913 during the Balkan Wars when many Jews fled from Turkey, Syria, the Balkan countries, and Greece. Monastir, now called Bitolj, is a city in southern Yugoslavia, and was an important center of Sephardic Jews. The immediate neighborhood was once populated with Levantine Jews; now there are virtually none left. Beyond a small faded sign hanging in front of the tenement, there is little to indicate the existence of a synagogue. One has to walk through the narrow dirt-littered hallway to a small room off the courtyard. At this writing, the small congregation has announced plans to abandon its diminutive synagogue and move to East Broadway where it can share more comfortable quarters with an Ashkenazic *chevra*.

(Letters correspond to location on map on page 40)

a. Adas Israel, 203 East Broadway
b. Agudas Chaverim Anshe Marmaros, 215 East Broadway
c. Anshe Lebedowe-Radzilowe, Lomze and Gatz, 225 East Broadway
d. Bnai Menashe Ahavas Achim, 229 East Broadway
e. Beth Hachasidim D'Polen, 233 East Broadway
f. Anshe Libovne-Valin, 237 East Broadway
g. Yeshuas Yacob Anshe Sfard, 239 East Broadway
h. Zemach Zedek Nusach Hoari, Bnai Avraham Anshe Chechanava, 241 East Broadway
i. Yitzchak Chasidei Boyon, 247 East Broadway
j. Beth Hamedrash Chasidei Belz, 255 East Broadway
k. Yeshuas Yacob-Anshe Horodetz, Anshe Viskave, Bakesh Shalom Anshe Ostrove, Anshe Szezcin and Anshe Grayewa, 257 East Broadway
l. Anshe Yendzhever and Bnai Moses Andrzievo, Mishkan Israel Anshei Zetel, 135 Henry Street
m. Ahavath Shalom Monastir, 133 Eldridge Street *(abandoned)*

OUR
EAST SIDE
COMMUNITY

MIKVAH

The First and Finest Ritualarium in the N. Y. Area

RENOVATED
AND
MODERNIZED

USE OUR MIKVAH REGULARLY—OBSERVE THE FUNDAMENTAL
REQUIRMENTS OF JEWISH FAMILY LIFE...

URGE YOUR FRIENDS AND NEIGHBORS TO OBSERVE JEWISH
FAMILY LIFE AS WELL...

SUPPORT OUR MIKVAH...

T'VILAS KAYLIM - IMMERSING UTENSILS . . .
Hours: SUNDAYS — 11:00 am to 1:00 pm / WEDNESDAYS — 1:00 to 2:00 pm

Kashrus of our mikvah is under the supervision of Rabbi Moshe Feinstein, Chairman of the Board

THE EAST SIDE MIKVAH
AGUDATH TAHARATH HA-MISHPOCHOH of the EAST SIDE, Inc.
311-13 EAST BROADWAY / NEW YORK, N.Y. 10002 / 475-8514

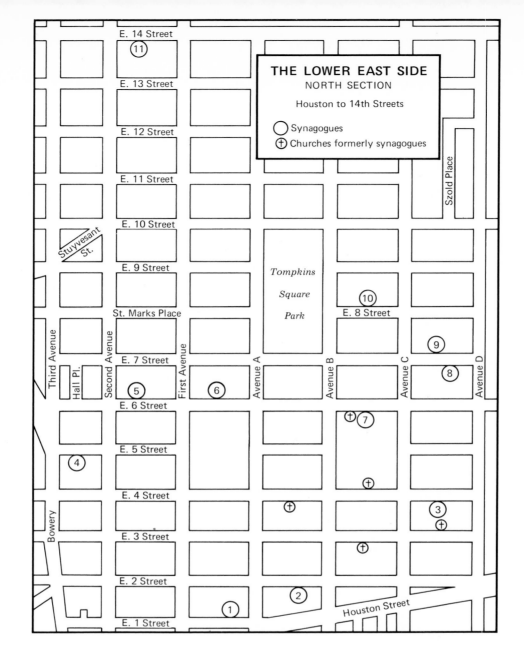

SMALL SYNAGOGUES NORTH OF HOUSTON STREET

(Numbers correspond to location on map)

1. Kochob Jacob Anshe Kamenetz Lite (Star of Jacob of the People of Kamenetz, Lithuania), 108 East 1st Street
2. Anshe Abatien (People of Abatien), 193 East 2nd Street *(demolished)*
3. Anshe Baranove (People of Baranove), 316 East 4th Street *(abandoned)*
4. Congregation Czernowitz-Bukoviner (Czernowitz and Bukovina), 224 East 5th Street
5. Community Synagogue, 325 East 6th Street
6. Adas Yisroel Anshe Mezeritch (Community of Israel of the People of Mezeritch), 415 East 6th Street
7. Ahavath Yeshurun Shara Torah (Love of Israel, Gates of the Torah), 638 East 6th Street *(abandoned)*
8. Beth Hamedrash Hagodol Anshe Ungarn (Great House of Study of the People of Hungary), 242 East 7th Street *(abandoned)*
9. Bnai Rappaport Anshe Rembrava (Sons of Rappaport, People of Rembrava) 207 East 7th Street *(abandoned)*
10. Bnai Moses Joseph Zavichost-Zosmer (Sons of Moses Joseph of Zavichost and Zosmer), 317 East 8th Street
11. Tifereth Israel (Glory of Israel), Town and Village Synagogue, 334 East 14th Street

THE SMALL SYNAGOGUES NORTH OF HOUSTON STREET

Only a few tiny enclaves and a small number of Jews remain north of Houston Street—a neighborhood which was once a vital part of the Lower East Side. Except for the fairly large Tifereth Israel (Glory of Israel) Congregation on East Fourteenth Street, a relatively young Conservative synagogue which calls itself the Town and Village Synagogue, only about half a dozen very small congregations survive. (The location of these synagogues is indicated on the map on page 142.) Each year witnesses the loss of more synagogues, through vandalism, arson, or the disappearance of the last few congregants. As this book goes to press, the Anshe Abatien Synagogue on East Second Street is being demolished by the city, since no owners of the building could be located. A few years ago the Bnai Menashe Synagogue on East Third Street was burned by neighborhood hoodlums, and the rabbi and congregants moved to a *shtiebl* at 229 East Broadway; their former *shul* was later purchased by a Spanish Pentecostal church. The old Lemburger Shul on East Fourth Street, with almost no supporting congregation left, sold the building to a Spanish Baptist congregation. In 1975, the ninety-year-old Congregation Anshe Baranove, also on East Fourth Street, was abandoned, as were Beth Hamedrash Hagodol Anshe Ungarn and Bnai Rappaport Anshe Rembrava, both on East Seventh Street.

Perhaps the most beautiful of all these small synagogues is Congregation Ahavath Yeshurun Shara Torah on East Sixth Street. It is a long narrow building with a gallery on three sides. The walls and ceiling are made of decorative sheet metal painted a dark color. The Ark, *bimah,* and gallery railings are of carved wood. A central round window with a huge *Mogen David* (Star of David) admits the only natural light. Three large brass candelabra hang low in the narrow space between the east and west galleries. At this writing it appears that the synagogue has closed its doors forever, joining the fate of its next-door neighbor, a former synagogue designed by the same architect and also built in the early 1890s which is now another Spanish church.

Another small *shul* with a most attractive interior is the little-used Adas Yisroel Anshe Mezeritch synagogue (Community of Israel of the People of Mezeritch) on East 6th Street. The unusually narrow building has balconies which extend almost to the middle of the sanctuary, and through the intervening space, broad rays of light from two overhead skylights seem to focus on the Ark and on a large stained glass panel above it. The soft-yellow-colored panes of the two-story-high window are crowned by an enormous *Mogen David* of red glass which seems to dominate the entire room. Sadly, it is only a matter of time until this little gem, named for a famous old center of Jewish learning in Poland, is added to the list of abandonments.

In the north section of the Lower East Side above Houston Street, there are only three congregations which can be considered active, and all are relative newcomers. The Community Synagogue was founded in 1940 and purchased the old St. Marks Lutheran Church at 325 East Sixth Street. Its lovely Greek Revival-style building adds a bit of charm to an otherwise drab neighborhood; its Greek portico with tall columns is reminiscent of America's second oldest synagogue, Beth Elohim, in Charleston, South Carolina.

Congregation Tifereth Israel (The Town and Village Synagogue) was organized in 1949 in the Sirovich Home for the Aged on Second Avenue near Fourteenth Street. The Conservative congregation then moved into the adjacent Labor Temple and shortly thereafter to a loft above a liquor store one block south. A permanent home was acquired when the congregation, in 1962, bought the neo-Romanesque-style building, topped by incongruous onion domes, of the Ukrainian Autocephalic Orthodox Church of St. Volodimir, at 334 East Fourteenth Street. Tifereth Israel draws most of its membership from the Stuyvesant Town and Peter Cooper Village housing complexes.

Congregation Kochob Jacob Anshe Kamenetz Lite (Star of Jacob, People of Kamenetz, Lithuania) at 108 East First Street, at the intersection of Houston Street, is of a design very typical of the 1920s, with its dark brown brick and simple, unadorned façade. It was erected in 1926 for Congregation Beth Haknesseth Anshe Padheitze (Synagogue of the People of Padheitze), and its survival is attributable to its fortunate location close to the Orchard Street business district and a cluster of neighboring apartment houses with a number of Jewish tenants. The name of the original Padheitze *chevra* is still visible above the arched entrance. An interesting later addition is the ornate iron gate presented by the "Ladies Auxiliary" with Yiddish lettering transliterated from English.

FORMER SYNAGOGUES

160

SOURCES

Cahan, Abraham. *The Rise of David Levinsky.* (Reprint of 1917 edition). New York: Harper & Row, 1966.

Glazer, Nathan. *American Judaism.* 2nd ed. University of Chicago Press, 1972.

Gold, Michael. *Jews without Money.* New York: Liveright, 1930.

Grinstein, Hyman B. *The Rise of the Jewish Community of New York, 1654–1860.* Philadelphia: Jewish Publication Society of America, 1945.

Hapgood, Hutchins. *The Spirit of the Ghetto.* (Reprint of 1902 edition). New York: Schocken Books, 1965.

Howe, Irving. *World of Our Fathers.* New York: Harcourt Brace Jovanovich, 1976.

Marcus, Jacob Rader. *Early American Jewry.* 2 vols. Philadelphia: Jewish Publication Society of America, 1951.

Metzger, Isaac, ed. *A Bintel Brief: Sixty Years of Letters from the Lower East Side to the* Jewish Daily Forward. Garden City, N.Y.: Doubleday, 1971.

Novotny, Ann. *Strangers at the Door.* Riverside, Conn.: Chatham Press, 1971.

Oppenheim, Samuel. *The Early History of the Jews in New York, 1654–1664.* Philadelphia: American Jewish Historical Society, no. 18 (1909).

Postal, Bernard, and Koppman, Lionel. *American Jewish Landmarks.* New York: Fleet Press, 1977.

Riis, Jacob A. *How the Other Half Lives.* (Reprint of 1903 edition). New York: Dover, 1971.

Rischin, Moses. *The Promised City.* Cambridge: Harvard University Press, 1962.

Sanders, Ronald. *The Downtown Jews: Portraits of an Immigrant Generation.* New York: Harper & Row, 1969.

Schoener, Allon, comp. *Portal to America: The Lower East Side 1870–1925.* New York: Holt, Rinehart and Winston, 1967.

Wischnitzer, Rachel. *Synagogue Architecture in the United States.* Philadelphia: Jewish Publication Society of America, 1955.

Wolfe, Gerard R. "The Lower East Side." In *New York: A Guide to the Metropolis,* chap. 6. New York: New York University Press, 1975.

LIST OF PHOTOGRAPHS

Page:

42 Congregation Khal Adas Jeshurun with Anshe Lubz

45 *Bimah* and sanctuary, Cong. Khal Adas Jeshurun with Anshe Lubz

46 Window panels, south wall, Cong. Khal Adas Jeshurun with Anshe Lubz

47 Benjamin Markowitz, *shammos,* Cong. Khal Adas Jeshurun with Anshe Lubz

48 Pew with old prayer books, Cong. Khal Adas Jeshurun with Anshe Lubz

49 Pew detail, Cong. Khal Adas Jeshurun with Anshe Lubz

50 Admonition sign from the *shammos,* Cong. Khal Adas Jeshurun with Anshe Lubz

51 Congregation Beth Hamedrash Hagodol

54 Welcome sign, Cong. Beth Hamedrash Hagodol

55 Rabbi Ephraim Oshry, Cong. Beth Hamedrash Hagodol

56 Sanctuary, Cong. Beth Hamedrash Hagodol

57 *Bimah* lamp, Cong. Beth Hamedrash Hagodol

58 Ritual ablution sinks, Cong. Beth Hamedrash Hagodol

59 Bialystoker Synagogue

61 Passover announcements and entrance to *bes medrash,* Bialystoker Synagogue

62 Hall and sanctuary, Bialystoker Synagogue

63 *(Above)* Detail, west window panels, *(below)* Detail, Ark and "Crown of the Law," Bialystoker Synagogue

64 *Bes medrash,* Bialystoker Synagogue

65 First Roumanian-American Congregation

67 Rabbi Mordecai Mayer, First Roumanian-American Congregation

69 Congregation Chasam Sopher

71   Congregant, Cong. Chasam Sopher

72   Entrance, Cong. Chasam Sopher

73   Ark, Cong. Chasam Sopher

74   Congregant at prayer, Cong. Chasam Sopher

75   Congregant at prayer, Cong. Chasam Sopher

76   Moses Weiser, President, Cong. Chasam Sopher

77   Prayer breakfast, Cong. Chasam Sopher

78   Alleyway door, Cong. Chasam Sopher

79   Congregation Beth Haknesseth Mogen Avraham and *(right)* Rozwadwer Synagogue

81   Carl Schiffer, President, at entrance, Cong. Beth Haknesseth Mogen Avraham

82   Entrance, Rozwadwer Synagogue

83   Rabbi Elias S. Heftler, Cong. Beth Haknesseth Mogen Avraham

84   Ephraim Heftler, son of Rabbi, Cong. Beth Haknesseth Mogen Avraham

85   Congregants, Cong. Beth Haknesseth Mogen Avraham

86   Reading the scroll of the Book of Esther at Purim, Cong. Beth Haknesseth Mogen Avraham

87   Reading the scroll of the Book of Esther at Purim, Cong. Beth Haknesseth Mogen Avraham

88   Picture on wall of *bes medrash,* Cong. Beth Haknesseth Mogen Avraham

89   Congregation Sons of Israel Kalwarie

91   *Bimah* and sanctuary, Cong. Sons of Israel Kalwarie

92   Israel Ginsberg, congregant, Cong. Sons of Israel Kalwarie

93   Israel Ginsberg at pulpit, Cong. Sons of Israel Kalwarie

94   Detail, west window panels, Cong. Sons of Israel Kalwarie

95   Congregation Anshe Slonim

98   Entrance, Cong. Anshe Slonim

99   Entrance door, Cong. Anshe Slonim

100 Sanctuary, Cong. Anshe Slonim

101 Ark, Cong. Anshe Slonim

102 Sanctuary, Cong. Anshe Slonim

104 Erste Warshawer Congregation

106 *Bimah* and sanctuary, Erste Warshawer Congregation

107 Pulpit and Ark, Erste Warshawer Congregation

108 Memorial plaques, Erste Warshawer Congregation

109 Window detail, Erste Warshawer Congregation

110 Sanctuary, Cong. Kehila Kadosha Janina
111 Congregation Kehila Kadosha Janina
112 *Bimah* and gallery, Cong. Kehila Kadosha Janina
113 Congregation Beth Haknesseth Etz Chaim Anshe Wolozin
114 House of Sages
115 Retired rabbis at prayer, House of Sages
116 House of Sages
117 House of Sages
118 Entrance, Cong. Senier and Wilno
119 Entrance, Cong. Senier and Wilno
120 Congregation Senier and Wilno (before damage by fire)
121 Congregation Senier and Wilno
123 Burning of leaven before Passover in front of Young Israel Synagogue.
124 East Side Torah Center
125 Erste Lutowisker Chevra
126 Downtown Talmud Torah Center
127 Congregation Bnai Jacob Anshe Brzezan
128 Rabbi Joseph Singer, Cong. Bnai Jacob Anshe Brzezan
129 *Bimah,* sanctuary, and gallery, Cong. Bnai Jacob Anshe Brzezan
130 Ritual ablution basin, Cong. Bnai Jacob Anshe Brzezan
131 South windows, Cong. Bnai Jacob Anshe Brzezan
132 *Shtieblach,* 255 and 257 East Broadway
136 *Shtiebl,* Chevra Mishkan Israel Anshei Zetel
137 *Shtiebl,* 257 East Broadway
138 *Shtiebl,* 241 East Broadway
139 *Shtiebl,* Ahavath Shalom Monastir
140 Advertisement for Ritualarium
141 Ritualarium
145 Congregation Anshe Baranove
146 Congregation Beth Hamedrash Hagodol Anshe Ungarn
147 Congregation Bnai Rappaport Anshe Rembrava
148 Congregation Ahavath Yeshurun Shara Torah, and *(right)* former synagogue, now a Spanish church
149 Congregation Adas Yisroel Anshe Mezeritch
150 Community Synagogue
151 Congregation Tifereth Israel–Town and Village Synagogue
152 Congregation Kochob Jacob Anshe Kamenetz Lite

171

153 Detail, entrance, Cong. Kochob Jacob Anshe Kamenetz Lite

154 Congregation Bnai Moses Joseph Zavichost-Zosmer

155 *Bes medrash,* Cong. Bnai Moses Joseph Zavichost-Zosmer

156 Interior, Cong. Bnai Moses Joseph Zavichost-Zosmer

157 Gallery, Cong. Bnai Moses Joseph Zavichost-Zosmer

160 Former synagogue of the Independent Kletzker Brotherly Aid Society, now the Zion Memorial Chapel and artist's residence above

161 Former Mishkan Israel Suwalki synagogue, now St. Barbara's Greek Orthodox Church

162 Former Anshe Ileya synagogue, now Union Square Seventh Day Adventist Church

163 Former Anshe Tifereth Jerushelaim synagogue, now Lincoln African Methodist Episcopal Church

164 Former *shtiebl,* Henry Street

165 Former synagogue, Hester Street